Creating a Reggio-Inspired STEM Environment for Young Children

Redleaf *Quick* Guide

Creating a Reggio-Inspired STEM Environment for Young Children

Vicki Carper Bartolini

Redleaf Press®
www.redleafpress.org
800-423-8309

Published by Redleaf Press
10 Yorkton Court
St. Paul, MN 55117
www.redleafpress.org

First edition 2021
Senior editor: Melissa York
Cover design by Renee Hammes
Cover photo by Anna Carper Bartolini
Typeset in Signo and Avenir by Douglas Schmitz
Interior photos by Rebecca Golding (pages 5 and 41), Michelle Curran-Mason (pages 16, 27, 46, 55, and 63), Deb Doucette (page 29), and Vicki Wright (page 65). All other photos by the author.
Printed in the United States of America
28 27 26 25 24 23 22 21   1 2 3 4 5 6 7 8

Library of Congress Cataloging-in-Publication Data

Names: Bartolini, Vicki Carper, author.
Title: Creating a Reggio-inspired STEM environment for young children / Vicki Carper Bartolini.
Description: First edition. | St. Paul, MN : Redleaf Press, 2021. | Includes bibliographical references and index. | Summary: "Award-winning educator Vicki Carper Bartolini offers practical suggestions and resources for rethinking your early learning environment with a focus on STEM, using the Reggio Emilia approach lens honoring a student-centered curriculum based on principles of respect, responsibility, and community through exploration and play"— Provided by publisher.
Identifiers: LCCN 2021007433 (print) | LCCN 2021007434 (ebook) | ISBN 9781605546988 (paperback) | ISBN 9781605546995 (ebook)
Subjects: LCSH: Reggio Emilia approach (Early childhood education) | Science—Study and teaching (Early childhood) | Technology—Study and teaching (Early childhood) | Student-centered learning.
Classification: LCC LB1029.R35 B37 2021 (print) | LCC LB1029.R35 (ebook) | DDC 372.21—dc23
LC record available at https://lccn.loc.gov/2021007433
LC ebook record available at https://lccn.loc.gov/2021007434

Printed on acid-free paper

To my curious and adventurous granddaughter Rosie (see the cover photo thanks to her mom, Anna) and to all young children everywhere who deserve wondrous, playful learning experiences.

CONTENTS

ACKNOWLEDGMENTS

I have so many to thank in bringing this book to fruition. Wheaton College in Massachusetts supported all my endeavors, from my trips to Reggio Emilia and Aotearoa New Zealand to an endowed faculty chair, allowing me precious time to work on the book. Receiving sabbatical funding from Patricia Arnold '66, trustee emerita, helped to fund my first transformative study trip to Reggio Emilia. The educators I met, visited, and heard speak during my trips there inspired all of my subsequent professional work, especially this book. I so appreciate and admire all the early childhood educators I have collaborated with and taught in courses who have challenged my thinking at every step of the way. A particular thank-you to Rebecca Golding, a former student and current teacher, for serving as my enthusiastic and dedicated research assistant. This book would not exist if it weren't for the endless discussions and generosity of preschool directors Michelle Curran-Mason of the Elisabeth Amen Nursery School, Deb Doucette of Head Start, and Vicki Wright of the Anchorage Park Kindergarten and their staffs. Melissa York, my skillful editor at Redleaf Press, made completion of the book seem deceptively easy. Finally, my family's loving encouragement and support throughout this project meant the world to me. Most especially, my husband, Bob Bartolini, deserves my deepest gratitude. Throughout my career, he has always had tremendous faith in me and pushed me, despite my many other obligations (and a pandemic!), to stay the course.

INTRODUCTION: LESSONS LEARNED FROM A PRESCHOOL TEACHER

We are living in a critical era in the evolution of early childhood education. We stand at the nexus of multiple areas of focus: the significant number of children in the United States spending literally years in early childhood education and care; the inequities in the accessibility, affordability, and quality of care in the programs children attend; the professional stresses facing early childhood educators; and the importance of creating high-quality playful learning environments for children. And in 2021, with the world in pandemic and the United States reckoning with systemic racism, these challenges felt ever more present.

Several streams of my long and treasured teaching career, working with both children and adults, flowed together to form my ever-evolving philosophy and ultimately led to the writing of this book. Earlier in my career, in my role as an elementary and special education teacher, I was committed to working with children who were challenged in one way or another, from complicated home lives to learning differences. Then in my role as an early childhood coordinator for a public school system, I became familiar with the challenges of working within what is often referred to as a "mixed delivery system" of early education and care (Marshall et al. 2005, 1)—that is, working with public, private, family child care, Head Start, early intervention, and school-age programs. Moving subsequently into higher education teacher preparation, both at the undergraduate and graduate levels, I worked with many future as well as experienced teachers all across New England.

During my time in higher education, I had the amazing opportunity to study multiple times in Reggio Emilia in northern Italy, internationally recognized for their exceptional early childhood programs. While there, I became enthralled with many aspects of their philosophy. I deeply admire not only their respect for the competencies of children, but also their regard for the intellectually stimulating work of early childhood educators. I observed that many of their famed child-centered projects integrated STEM experiences. For example, I attended a presentation documenting children's inquiry and research into how to create a rainbow. Other well-known projects include children's study of birds and the construction of an amusement park for the birds. I was particularly inspired by their appreciation for the importance of the learning environment and their conception of the environment as "the third teacher" in the classroom.

Afterward, combining my interests in providing high-quality early education and care for all children, learning through play, early STEM literacy, and the Reggio Emilia philosophy, I began video documentation projects of young children as they developed early STEM understandings through play across a variety of settings. Ultimately, this STEM focus led to a publication in *Innovations in Early Education: The International Reggio Emilia Exchange*, national and international conference presentations, and my commitment not only to teaching but to advocacy and policy work on behalf of all young children and early childhood educators.

During our current turbulent times, these priorities still drive my work. Although, as I am writing this, we do not yet know what a post-COVID preschool education will look like, we as a society are beginning to recognize more than ever the essential role of early education not only to the benefit of our children but also to the viability of our economy. Additionally, we are in desperate need of learners who value inquiry and STEM, ultimately becoming STEM-literate citizens and, in some cases, STEM professionals. We must resolve to make access to high-quality early education and care equitable for all children, including Black children, Indigenous children, and children of color who are often left behind in our patched-together mixed delivery system of early education and care. Regardless of socioeconomic status, gender, race, ethnicity, disability, religion, or first language, all children deserve opportunities to develop their competencies. All children deserve programs staffed with caring and well-prepared educators. All children deserve stimulating learning environments where inquiry through play is valued. Subsequently, as a society, we are starting to better appreciate the essential work of well-prepared early educators and the importance of high-quality early education and care.

As policy makers and administrators push STEM education more and more, increased support for teachers' professional development is essential. Thus, this book was born out of years of experience with children, teachers, administrators, and policy makers and the pressing need to provide high-quality early STEM learning environments for all children. For several years, I taught a course to preschool teachers interested in integrating STEM into their settings. I met "Marie," a preschool teacher who intrigued (and initially frustrated) me with her attitude toward my course, Teaching Preschool STEM. To learn more about the teachers, I asked them their goals for the course. Whereas some talked about wanting to understand inquiry more deeply, gain familiarity with new state standards, or learn more about the Reggio Emilia schools, Marie told me she "just" wanted to know what materials she should have in her classroom environment. At the time, I thought that together the other students and I could answer her question during the first session. I was puzzled that this was "all" she wanted out of the course, given that her center seemed to be well resourced.

What I soon realized was how important her question was to my understanding of these teachers' needs and how honest and brave Marie was for asking this question. The teachers' needs were abundant, including

- understanding inquiry and the scientific processes involved in STEM,

- developing content knowledge of topics,

- identifying and accessing appropriate professional resources,

- implementing prescribed activities while supporting learning through guided play,

- building background knowledge,

- preparing to teach in new ways,

- and perhaps most importantly, finding professional time and garnering administrative support to accomplish these goals.

This was an aha moment for me in how to better collaborate with preschool teachers to meet their practical and urgent needs. After all, they were working while at the same time trying to strengthen their own STEM background knowledge, acquire necessary materials, set up their learning environments, and teach the wonder of STEM playfully and effectively to young children—a tall order indeed! These are the same preschool teachers whom our society has come to rely on to support our workforce, yet these "essential workers" are typically over-worked, underpaid, and devalued.

Ultimately, Marie's efforts, and those of her colleagues in the class, far surpassed my expec-tations. Their projects showcased young children's studies of sound, states of matter, shadows and light, construction/design of buildings, and gardening, as well as documenta-tion of teachers' developing questioning skills. Teachers reported making changes to their preschool environment, including more inquiry-based learning and less prescriptive teaching. Others shared how they were using the outdoors as a classroom, not just a playground, or how they were stretching more focused studies over days and weeks, rather than squeezing in fifteen- to twenty-minute STEM activities. Others shared strategies they used to advocate for support from directors and communicate their efforts to families.

Through my experience with Marie and interactions with thousands of other preschool teachers, I've come to the conclusion that *Creating a Reggio-Inspired STEM Environment for Young Children* needs to focus on these key practical yet philosophical issues:

- messages and values in the early childhood STEM setting

- use of time, use of space, aesthetics, materials

- the teacher's role

Use of these elements also promotes the 6Cs as described by Roberta Golinkoff and Kathy Hirsh-Pasek in their book *Becoming Brilliant* (2016): collaboration, communication, content, critical thinking, creative innovation, and confidence. These authors agree that the "Reggio way" encourages the greatest joy, satisfaction, and intellectual engagement for both the child and the teacher. My hope is that starting small, one step at a time, readers will begin to reimagine a playful and inquiry-based STEM learning environment, welcoming of all children, that is inviting, magical, and full of wonder.

How to Use This Book

Readers will find that each chapter focuses on one element to consider in designing a playful, inquiry-based preschool STEM learning environment. Chapter 1, "Lessons Learned from Reggio Emilia," highlights tenets of the Reggio Emilia philosophy that have profoundly impacted my work with preschool teachers. Chapter 2 focuses on messages and values in the STEM environment. Readers consider how their expertise in setting up the prereading environment reveals their values to children and families. They then will compare the messages and values expressed in their prereading environment to those conveyed in their STEM learning environment.

Chapters 3 and 4 focus on the flexible use of space and time to promote and sustain STEM studies, often lacking in US preschool settings. Chapter 5, "Aesthetics," encourages the reader to contemplate the importance of beauty, order, and natural elements. In chapter 6, "Materials and Themes," I share a sampling of STEM studies and corresponding materials to have on hand. "The Teacher's Role in the STEM-Centered Learning Environment," chapter 7, encourages the reader to consider what is referred to as the "pedagogy of listening" in Reggio centers, as well as other aspects of teachers' knowledge and skills. Finally, the book ends with a sampling of exemplary resources that preschool teachers and I have found beneficial in designing the STEM learning environment.

A practical feature included in each chapter is a **Self-Assessment Checklist** to help the reader decide on **One Thing to Try Tomorrow**. Each chapter closes with **Snapshots** of three different preschools—each with varying degrees of flexibility, finances, and support—in their ongoing journeys to address challenges big and small in their STEM learning environments. The Elisabeth Amen Nursery School on the Wheaton College campus, a Head Start program local to the author, and the Anchorage Park Kindergarten in Auckland, Aotearoa New Zealand, provide snapshots of evolving STEM learning environments influenced by the Reggio Emilia philosophy. The Elisabeth Amen Nursery School finds that its journey has primarily focused on creating an outdoor classroom. The Head Start program works to balance prescribed curriculum with more playful, inquiry-based STEM studies. And the Anchorage Park Kindergarten continues its efforts to create a magical environment that is respectful of all children's competencies.

Throughout, the book emphasizes the importance of including *all* children in the STEM learning environment, regardless of gender, race, ethnicity, religion, first language, disability, or socioeconomic status. Additionally, it is our responsibility as teachers to model respect for our planet by using low-cost (or no-cost) recycled and repurposed materials. It is also our obligation to nurture children's appreciation and responsibility for the natural world of which we are all a part.

And, finally, when reading this book, and always: be patient with yourself. Change takes time. Start small with a baby step, test it out, and see what works and doesn't work for your setting. Find others to work with, laugh with, and wonder with!

CHAPTER 1:
LESSONS LEARNED
FROM REGGIO EMILIA

And our expectations of the child must be very flexible and varied. We must be able to be amazed and to enjoy, like the children often do. We must be able to catch the ball that the children throw us, and toss it back to them in a way that makes the children want to continue the game with us, developing, perhaps, other games as we go along.

—Tiziana Filippini, pedagogista and former director of the Documentation and Research Centre, Reggio Emilia, quoted in *The Hundred Languages of Children*, 3rd ed.

As with thousands of others who have been inspired by the Reggio philosophy, my thinking about the environment, particularly as it relates to STEM learning, transformed all of my professional work. I was surprised to notice how many of the Reggio investigations I observed or read about involve inquiry-based STEM learning. Whether children are studying the architecture of the buildings in their city or the mechanics of the curtains in a theater, they are consistently engaged in the 6Cs while conducting observations, collecting data, making predictions, and analyzing and evaluating data. Capturing children's questions, assumptions, collaborations, misunderstandings, communications, revisions, findings, joy, and wonder as they experimented with the properties of water, gears and mechanical devices, and the chemical processes of cooking reinforced my thinking about children's competencies and the importance of access to high-quality, playful learning experiences.

All children deserve wondrous, stimulating, and creative STEM learning environments where their amazements, curiosities, questions, and observations are valued. At the same time, all teachers deserve the opportunity and support to create such learning environments, ones that are inspiring and inviting to them as well. What I call "the Reggio way" provides a road map as to how this might be done, with emphasis on finding one thing to try tomorrow using everyday, low-cost (or no-cost), thoughtfully chosen materials. Throughout this book, I focus on the following elements that are central to my understanding of the Reggio philosophy:

1. Teachers in Reggio Emilia describe the classroom environment as the "third teacher."

Typically preschool classrooms are staffed by two adults who scaffold and facilitate learning. In these early childhood Reggio centers, the environment is considered the third teacher, the laboratory where learning is supported and constructed. The intentional design of this environment fosters encounters, relationships, communication, and collaboration among children and adults. Provocations such as puzzling objects or items from nature spur surprise, wonder, curiosity, discussion, and further study. Children's questions and interests evolve into investigations alongside their teachers. In this instructional and flexible space, studies unfold over time. Natural light, the color palette, and the careful selection and placement of materials create an inspiring instructional environment. Panels of children's work reflect respect and trust in children's competencies. The reader will find further discussion of the messages and values embedded in the environment (chapter 2), the use of time (chapter 3), the use of space (chapter 4), aesthetics (chapter 5), and the choice of materials (chapter 6).

2. Teachers in Reggio often describe their work with children as *inquiry* or *research*.

Practicing a "pedagogy of listening" prompted by children's questions and interests, teachers collaboratively engage in investigations using scientific processes, or the inquiry method—what some in the United States call *project-based learning*. Together they make observations, gather information, analyze the data, propose solutions, and reflect on their new learning. Viewing the children as competent and capable, full of intelligence, the teachers trust that children can sustain their engagement with complex, child-generated topics over a period of time. Children collaborate to research a topic or problem of interest, coming up with their own ideas. Along the way, while listening to children, teachers provoke further curiosity and critical thinking by asking open-ended questions. Together teachers and children document the learning process and outcomes of their investigations, capturing aha moments for reflection and celebration (chapter 7). Some examples of inquiry-based or project-based learning include planting and tending a garden, cooking with vegetables and fruits, composting with worms, and observing and recording life cycles of plants and animals.

3. In creating a Reggio-inspired learning environment, teachers promote the 6Cs.

As described in *Becoming Brilliant* by Roberta Golinkoff and Kathy Hirsh-Pasek (2016), the 6Cs are collaboration, communication, content, critical thinking, creativity, and confidence. As the authors note, "In many ways, the Reggio approach to learning is a perfect example of the 6Cs at work in a school environment. Like the 6Cs, it was born from the science that views children not just as heads but as whole, active engaged people with social sides too" (264). In the Reggio-inspired environment, children collaborate and communicate as they plan a project that provides for the study of rich content. Using their creative and critical-thinking skills—observing, comparing and contrasting, predicting, analyzing, reflecting—they investigate their topic. Despite probable bumps and disagreements along the way, they build self-confidence, trust, and respect for one another as they satisfactorily document, complete, and share their investigation or project.

4. Teachers lead by example.

Throughout this book, I have sprinkled my beliefs about how important it is that we inspire children to marvel at, value, and care for the sacred web of life. Reggio educators strive to bring the outdoors in and the indoors out, understanding the learning opportunities found in nature. This commitment continues with their responsible and innovative use of the Remida, the Creative Recycling Centre. Here industries donate unused or scrap materials that teachers recycle and repurpose.

Self-Assessment Checklist

- What is the philosophy of your setting? Classroom? Preschool? Do you have a philosophy? How might the Reggio elements discussed in this book and the 6Cs connect with you or help you develop and make visible a living, breathing philosophy?

- What resources do you already have that you can build upon? What interesting materials might be available? Perhaps you have access to a safe neighborhood for outdoor adventures. Are you within walking distance of a park, library, museum, factory, pond, shady trees, or open field? Do you have parents, colleagues, or friends who might be willing to share their hobbies or expertise in STEM areas?

Snapshot: Elisabeth Amen Nursery School

The historic Elisabeth Amen Nursery School, situated on the campus of Wheaton College in Norton, Massachusetts, provides a private full and part-day preschool program. It serves as a lab for the psychology department and field placement site for the education department. Following a study trip with me to Reggio Emilia, the former director of the nursery school returned to this campus lab school questioning the "old scripts" and the messages and values promoted in the environment of their early childhood program. Her questioning was the start to many changes in the nursery school, continuing today with a passionate new director (a teacher who worked with the former director). For example, the entrance hallway (or what in Reggio would be considered a kind of piazza) is now valued as a place of intersection and social exchange for passing teachers, staff, children, parents, and college students who work at the nursery school. Documentation of the children's investigations is showcased, promoting public discussion as passersby notice, question, interpret, and admire children's work.

As the new director proudly notes, their entrance to the school conveys "respect for the child" and "the wonder of it all," very much in keeping with the Reggio philosophy as well as with the 6Cs. However, as she notes, "Change is a process that takes time. It involves staff buy-in, figuring out things together, being afraid yet still taking risks, testing and revisiting, and of course finding resources." They have found that establishing some long-term goals while working on one short-term objective at a time helps them to maintain balance and perspective. Since 2014, their overarching long-term goal has been to transform their traditional playground into a playful outdoor, inquiry-based classroom, while also working to integrate the arts with inquiry-based learning (what some might call STEAM—science, technology, engineering, arts, and mathematics). Short-term objectives allow the parent advisory committee, in place for a two-year commitment, to focus their energies on a specific project while working toward the overarching long-term goal. Objectives have included purchasing a four-sided outdoor easel and providing a cover for the outside stage for children's presentations. Working together on the outdoor classroom has forged a great partnership among families, local volunteers, and the staff. Snapshots of the Amen Nursery School throughout this book primarily focus on the ongoing development of their outdoor STEM learning environment.

Snapshot: Local Head Start Program

At the local Head Start, the director noted that STEM is now everywhere in the environment. Opportunities for hands-on exploration can be found all around the setting, including bookcases, shelves, the dramatic play area, in displays of children's books, and outdoors. Teachers have made STEM tools such as scales, magnifying glasses, large magnets, blocks, and tweezers readily accessible for hands-on explorations. Children's observations of life cycles are at eye level, encouraging questions, discussion, data analysis, and conclusions.

Comprehensive in its offerings, this part-day federally funded preschool program includes education, nutrition, medical, family support, transportation, and home visiting components. Children come from many backgrounds, often from families whose first language is not English. Entry into the program is based on income criteria. As a federal program, they must follow extensive regulations, including use of the required Creative Curriculum. A few years ago, Head Start programs began to emphasize the integration of STEM studies and experiences for children. Although the local Head Start program did not intentionally design their current program based on knowledge of the Reggio Emilia philosophy, they have found that, over time, they are uncovering and embracing many Reggio elements as they work to implement their curricular guidelines.

A few years ago, working with Wheaton College students, the director began a weekly STEM Day. College students planned and implemented the weekly activities. The director now describes STEM as having become more integrated, in "little ways" throughout each day, with the teachers and children no longer seeing "today" as STEM Day. She describes the teachers as becoming more excited and finding the integration of STEM "not that hard." In fact, she describes the children as often leading the teachers—evidence of teachers listening to children and co-researching with them, principle elements of a Reggio approach, as when teachers and children investigated prisms, light, and rainbows together. And in true Reggio style, at the end of many blocks of study, a community celebration with children, families, and teachers takes place.

~~~~~~

Snapshot: Anchorage Park Kindergarten

The Anchorage Park Kindergarten staff fosters an "engaging magical environment" where the environment is the third teacher. Children move seamlessly from the outdoors to the indoors, exploring with wonder and curiosity while engaging in the 6Cs.

This award-winning, publicly funded kindergarten serves preschool children and their families in a suburban area of Auckland in both full- and part-day programs. Following Te Whāriki, the Aotearoa New Zealand early childhood education curriculum that reflects both English and Maori cultures, the center also meets the policies of the local kindergarten association. However, as the head teacher explains, "Each kindergarten has its own philosophy, vision, and business plan allowing for their personal beliefs about teaching and learning, social competencies, culture, and community to shine." Anchorage Park's process of change began in mid-2009, when making one small change using clay and art naturally evolved as the team began to ask, "How do we provide a magical space for children and change our environment to uphold our philosophy? How do we change to provoke children's thought processes? How do we ignite that spark? How does our environment meet children's needs? How do we balance all their needs?" These profound questions triggered the process to create an "engaging magical environment."

The head teacher visited four centers that reflect the Reggio Emilia philosophy, each one more amazing than the last. She contacted an expert to serve as their mentor during this change process. The mentor provoked their thinking, challenging them to succinctly explain the essence of their center's philosophy. Six months later, after much in-house dialogue, they were able to identify their philosophy in four powerful sentences. They found that change came "one little piece at a time" and that the process of change provoked strengths in the teaching team.

"We learned to trust our team strengths, our thought processes and beliefs, and to stand tall," very much in keeping with the way Reggio educators see their work as democratically inspired and intellectually stimulating. Long-term sustainable goals, reflecting the needs of their fifty families and nineteen cultures, remain their priority to this day.

CHAPTER 2:
MESSAGES AND VALUES
IN THE STEM ENVIRONMENT

The concept of the "environment as the third teacher" continues to be developed. . . . We have begun to realize that this concept is much more complex than any set of guidelines for appropriate equipment, materials, room arrangement, and display. It is tied to our image of the child; knowledge and ongoing study of any given group of children, teachers, and parents; our understanding of the concept of scaffolding; our use of documentation; and our ways of thinking about organization of time and relations among all members of the learning community.

—Brenda Fyfe in *Reflections on the Reggio Emilia Approach*

Many preschool teachers spend countless hours intentionally designing the optimal prereading/early literacy learning environment. For example, walking into my local Head Start program, parents and children are immediately greeted by children's names adorning cubbies and birthday charts. Carefully written labels in English and Spanish (and sometimes additional languages) are strategically placed on furniture to encourage connections between print and objects. An inviting writing table is covered with recycled paper and envelopes, rubber stamps, fat and skinny markers, pencils and pens to foster purposeful "writing." A cozy reading corner is outfitted with carpet, fluffy pillows, and a rocking chair. Color-coded bins, intentionally developed and organized with great sophistication, contain picture books, theme-based books, fiction and nonfiction books, multicultural books, books on tape, and books in languages other than English. Nearby is a puppet theater with store-bought and handmade puppets for children to act out stories. Looking across the setting, families often see parents, grandparents, and student volunteers reading to children. They see the teacher recording children's words as they describe their paintings or block structures, or helping to write birthday cards. The alphabet is displayed at children's eye level, and the easel holds an inviting big book. Parents notice special backpacks containing books that families are encouraged to take home and read aloud nightly. This is a small sample of the sophisticated knowledge base and pedagogical strategies teachers employ in designing and developing a stimulating early prereading environment.

This description also speaks volumes regarding the values and messages these Head Start educators choose to convey in their classroom learning environments. Through their intentional choices, parents and children perceive that prereading literacy is important, social, stimulating, inviting, and relaxing. There are multiple entry points. You can do it alone or with a friend. There isn't always a "right or wrong" way, and there are many opportunities to practice. Different cultures and family structures are respected through the choices of children's books. The 6Cs—communication, collaboration, content, creativity, critical thinking, and confidence—are promoted through the prereading opportunities in the environment.

Messages and Values in the Preschool STEM Environment

Preschool teachers in my Teaching Preschool STEM course reflect on what messages and values their environments convey about the importance of inquiry and early STEM learning. To kick-start this reflection, we begin where they feel most comfortable—brainstorming how they currently set up their learning environments to reinforce the importance of prereading skills. The list is typically exhaustive and confidently created as most preschool teachers are quite passionate and clear about their beliefs and knowledgeable when it comes to promoting the prereading environment. We then do a similar exercise in setting up an inquiry-based and playful STEM learning environment. This activity is usually more challenging as many teachers struggle to articulate the extent to which STEM learning is prioritized and integrated across their settings. Comparing and contrasting the two lists provokes further discussion about why the prereading list was easier to complete than the STEM environment list. This analysis and reflection leads many educators to aha moments: most likely, given their difficulty with the exercise, they are not broadcasting an intentional message about the importance of STEM for families or children, often reflecting the teacher's lack of confidence and expertise in STEM content (as opposed to prereading) or an ill-defined philosophy about the importance of early STEM literacy.

Reimagining the STEM Learning Environment

As our class discusses this further, we begin to imagine a STEM learning environment that employs Reggio principles and the 6Cs, contrasting this with what these preschool teachers typically offer in the setup of STEM environments. For example, in an environment that conveys the importance of inquiry-based STEM learning, children work together in playful investigations, conveying the importance of the social aspects of STEM (communication, collaboration, and so on). Perhaps children are excitedly sharing binoculars as they begin a study of birds perching at bird feeders. Observing and discussing the variety of colors and sizes of birds outside the window, they document what they see, using drawings, sculptures, photos, or videos. They explore books and videos to identify the birds, capturing their data on a chart. In contrast, teachers in the course acknowledge that instead of promoting and providing flexible time for children's inquiry, they more often place a salvaged bird's nest on the windowsill alongside some bird books and a poster of different kinds of birds, hoping the children notice.

In our imagined STEM learning environment, documentation panels of children's STEM studies are visible, allowing children and families to revisit, reflect, and celebrate their learning. For example, panels of photos capture the children's building projects, including a study of tools and simple machines. However, teachers admit that they rarely preserve lasting evidence of STEM activities or investigations to showcase children's learning. Instead of responding to the children's interests and prodding their critical thinking with open-ended questioning and co-researching answers alongside them, more often than not the teachers either provide the right answers, correct the wrong responses, or allow misconceptions to go unchallenged, especially if they lack confidence in their own STEM knowledge.

This exercise, comparing and contrasting an imagined STEM learning environment with the realities and challenges of many preschool environments, leads the class to plan how to thoughtfully integrate STEM across the curriculum and *intentionally* convey messages and values to children and families. Using course readings from my studies in Reggio Emilia, STEM video documentation from my own work in early childhood settings, discussion of the 6Cs, and the self-assessment checklists from this book, we spend much of the course reimagining the messages and values that teachers' STEM learning environments might intentionally convey.

Given their budding self-awareness, teachers commit to an ambitious, yet doable, plan for the duration of the course (and hopefully beyond). It's also my hope that you, too, as the reader of this book will find inspiration from their experiences that will impact your work. They agree to develop and articulate their STEM environment philosophy, considering influences from Reggio educators as well as the 6Cs. Using the Self-Assessment Checklist and One Thing to Try Tomorrow exercises, they identify and commit to tackling small changes within their settings. Finally, they plan to implement and document at least one longer-term STEM investigation, based on their children's questions and interests. Participants are encouraged to work together if at all possible to benefit from one another's perspectives and for mutual encouragement and support. At periodic check-ins, each participant brings documentation (notes on index cards, outlines, drawings, photos, samples of children's work, videos, and so on) to class to share evidence, celebrate success, and seek feedback on their ongoing efforts. This collaborative, Reggio-style professional development fosters reflection, problem solving, and, most importantly, celebration of progress.

Teachers consider several questions as starting points in developing their own philosophical perspectives:

- How important is STEM literacy? Do you believe STEM literacy is important to your own life as a teacher and citizen?

- Do you feel a responsibility for children to regularly engage in STEM learning? If so, do you model the dispositions of curiosity, wonder, surprise, bewilderment, and so on?

- Do you see all children as capable STEM learners?

- Is your setting accessible to those with adaptive equipment requirements?

- Are all genders, Indigenous children, and children of color encouraged and supported in your STEM play and investigations?

- Are labels for STEM items, books, and videos presented in multiple languages to support English learners?

- Do opportunities for investigations vary in complexity to accommodate a range of learning abilities?

- Do you see inquiry as central to children's STEM learning? Do you listen to children's questions and interests and ask open-ended questions?

- How are the 6Cs prioritized as central to STEM learning?

- Is guided play considered a learning opportunity?

- Do children always need to find the right answer?

- How can flexible space, indoors and out, as well as the flexible use of time support investigations?

- Does the setting promote curiosity and wonder?

- How can you model responsibility toward the natural environment for children?

Slowly and thoughtfully transitioning to a more inquiry-based STEM environment requires careful consideration and selection of materials (my student Marie's original question!). Are recycled and repurposed items valued and available? Is recycling promoted? Are natural materials (pebbles, leaves, shells, pine cones), simple machines (pulleys, levers, gears), transportation items (trucks, cars, boats, planes, bikes), living items (plants, animals), loose parts (beads, buttons, screws, mirrors, odds and ends), ramps, balls, blocks, and tools (binoculars, funnels, tubes, tweezers) available and easily accessible?

Teachers also informally assess whether families, children, colleagues, and administrators notice their more intentional values and messages surrounding STEM learning. Parents might see children engaged in guided play or playful learning. In *A Mandate for Playful Learning in Preschool*, Hirsh-Pasek, Golinkoff, Berk, and Singer state, "Playful learning or guided play actively engages children in pleasurable and seemingly spontaneous activities that encourage academic exploration and learning. . . . With playful learning, children are not searching for one right answer or wandering freely about the classroom without supervision. Rather, the children feel free to explore while the teacher makes sure they encounter certain content" (2009, 54). These playful investigations might include creating an invention with loose parts, constructing props for a theatrical production, preparing a variety of snacks for a celebration, building with blocks to make the fastest delivery route for trucks traveling through the mountains, across the river, to the city, and so on. Parents might also see children engaging in the 6Cs just as real scientists and engineers do—conjecturing, disagreeing, challenging, negotiating, demonstrating, and sharing strategies while grappling with ambiguity, frustration, mistakes, and misconceptions.

Parents begin to notice that high-quality early STEM learning experiences involve collaborative and playful social interactions coupled with learning through trial and error or risk-taking. Through these social exchanges, children listen to and learn strategies from each other. Those with limited background experiences engage in problem solving alongside others with more varied experiences. Children learning to speak English play with their friends and, alongside them, learn new vocabulary. STEM is actively integrated throughout the setting, not passively isolated to a display on a shelf or windowsill. Graphs, charts, tables, and posters capture children's growing understanding of data collection and analysis. Teachers model the pedagogy of listening, respecting children's questions and interests while responding with open-ended questions. Living things and life cycles are observable both inside and out, while natural materials abound for careful observation, sorting, and admiring. The outdoors is viewed as another classroom where curiosity, respect, and care for the natural world are nurtured. The playful, magical, and wondrous STEM learning environment, much like a prereading learning environment, not only recognizes the competencies of all children but also incorporates the essential elements of flexible time and space, aesthetic qualities, carefully chosen materials, and full realization of the environment's role as the third teacher.

As the teachers in my course work to design a more intentional, provocative, and stimulating STEM environment, we discuss the values and messages they hope to convey to children and families through their choices.

Self-Assessment Checklist

- Is STEM limited to a science center, table, windowsill, or shelf, or are STEM opportunities and materials integrated throughout my setting?

- Are children talking and working in groups, conducting experiments with such items as balls and ramps, lights and shadows, magnets, and so forth?

- Is there documentation or photos of groups of children engaged in collaborative inquiry about bubbles, plants, puddles, life cycles, and so forth?

- Are developmentally appropriate yet content-rich nonfiction books and photos about topics such as weather, life cycles, simple machines, transportation, counting, and so forth available for children's investigations and research?

- Are there plants (and realistic photos of plants) in various stages of development for observing, predicting, and recording in journals or with cameras? Are there terrariums for studying life cycles and the water cycle?

- Are there natural materials (pieces of wood, stones, shells, and so forth) and synthetic materials (beads, buttons, toy figures and cars, and so forth) available for organizing or tinkering?

- Are there charts and graphs posted to support children's investigations?

- Are there outdoor gardens for composting, planting, weeding, harvesting, and recording observations? (In limited spaces, mini-gardens can be planted in large pots or bins.) Are there bird feeders, binoculars, and bird books for observing and researching birds, as well as cameras, drawing paper, and markers for recording data?

- Are there opportunities for building structures outside or for playing in sand, water, and mud?

- Are there quiet, intimate, inviting places, both indoors and out, for collaboration, reflection, and relaxation while imaginatively playing with ideas?

- How do the messages in the environment convey respect for all of life and the importance of taking care of our planet? Do you reuse, repurpose, and recycle materials?

- How is technology used? Is it primarily used as a tool for researching topics of interest while actively involving children in the 6Cs?

- Are teachers listening to children's questions and comments while modeling the important dispositions of curiosity, wonder, skepticism, surprise, and so forth?

- Are all children involved and viewed as capable and competent, including those who need specialized equipment, navigable space, or attention to language development, and so forth? Are girls, Indigenous children, and children of color fully supported to participate and challenge themselves?

One Thing to Try Tomorrow

Consider inviting an enthusiastic colleague or mentor to join you—someone you respect and trust who is also interested in the STEM learning environment. Take out your phone or tablet and slowly pan your setting. Together, play back the video for reflection (and probably some laughter too). Without judgment, ask yourself and your colleague: What jumps out as the messages and values in your environment? What do you and your colleague notice regarding STEM? Do you see STEM as a priority that is well integrated across your setting? If your evolving philosophy about the importance of the STEM environment is not as apparent as you would like, review the Self-Assessment Checklist to determine a starting point for slowly transitioning into a more Reggio-inspired STEM environment that promotes playful and joyful learning. Give yourself a pat on the back for taking this small but important step!

Snapshot: Elisabeth Amen Nursery School

Focusing on the outdoor classroom, seasonal STEM investigations at the Amen Nursery School include walking through the apple orchard, apple picking, tasting, graphing, and cooking, as well as planning, planting, and tending the vegetable garden. Many opportunities arise for children to collaborate and communicate while they are involved in life science studies.

This preschool has long embraced a play-based curriculum. With reflection, ongoing study, and professional development, the staff worked to more clearly articulate and make visible to children, families, and the community their philosophy and values through the intentional choices they made in redesigning the environment. The Reggio principles of time, space, choice of materials, and outdoor learning, along with the importance of the 6Cs, were made more apparent. Changes to the outdoor environment show its central role in their emergent and project-based life sciences curriculum. Bird feeders, placed right outside the classroom windows, provide endless opportunities for observation and research. Seasonal STEM investigations include apple picking, tasting, graphing, and cooking, as well as planning, planting, and tending the vegetable garden. Learning about life cycles, children conduct a worm study, examine pond life, and explore what the children refer to as the "magical woods" on campus—a woodsy spot that is a little dark and mysterious and also full of surprising plant and animal life. Recently the staff, families, and Wheaton students collaborated on building an outdoor mud kitchen.

Snapshot: Local Head Start Program

As children, families, and visitors walk into this Head Start program after two years of ongoing change, messages about the importance of STEM in the early childhood environment are visible everywhere. Though each classroom is unique, the integrated nature of STEM is embedded in big and little ways throughout the center. For example, while one teacher is working with children on a roads and transportation study, another teacher and her children are conducting a tree study. The ongoing, complex study of roads and transportation entails block constructions spread out over a fairly large area with toy workers, signs, equipment, and various kinds of trucks. Children glue cutout paper triangles, circles, squares, and rectangles to create different kinds of trucks while also exploring shapes. Resources include posters, photographs, and children's books. Meanwhile, the tree study explores tree cookies, wood shavings, and bark in the water/sand table and includes walks to the nearby college campus nature trail to compare and contrast kinds of trees and to track changes in trees over time. Children's books focusing on STEM topics and tools such as binoculars, magnifying glasses, magnets, and balance scales are easily accessible throughout the classrooms. Though their studies are implemented as part of the required curriculum, extended investigations emerge from the teachers' or the children's questions and interests.

As the director notes, "The teachers place importance on the children's experiences." Valuing diverse perspectives, they allow children's questions to drive these extended investigations beyond the required curriculum when possible. Sharing her observations of their study about changing seasons, she noted that some children from countries outside the United States had never seen trees that change colors or felt snow, so the classroom teacher invited them to share about their familiar environments and ecosystems. This led to the class exploring what else, in addition to trees, might live and grow there. Contrasting and comparing in this way encourages children's critical thinking while building a collective body of knowledge. Children still learning English were explaining to their new friends (with help from the teacher and their peers) the differences between what the class observed and what the children might see if they visited their home countries. These discussions engaged the children in communicating with one another about their experiences with the rich content of living things (plants and animals) and seasonal variations (leaves changing and snow).

Snapshot: Anchorage Park Kindergarten

Creating small, intimate, and "private" spaces conveys the Anchorage Park Kindergarten's belief in the competencies of children to imagine, reflect, wonder, and communicate while relaxing alone or with others. Designing with interesting fabrics and patterns, sheer drapery, wind chimes, and books creates the inviting time and space for curious minds to ponder!

To ensure that the messages and values of their newly articulated philosophy were visible to the children, families, and staff, the Anchorage Park Kindergarten team spent a professional development week emptying out their center of all furniture and materials. They examined each item, asking themselves, "How does this reflect our philosophy? Is it needed? Does it reflect the inclusive, high-quality program that we envision? Does it contribute to an environment that nurtures social competence and a sense of belonging? Does it promote inquiry learning? Does it create small learning spaces for dialogue and interaction?" Some items were returned to the reimagined setting while others were donated to families or other programs.

The Anchorage Park Kindergarten environment has evolved over the past several years into a school visited by others (including the author!) to learn about the opportunities that abound in such an inspiring, magical environment. It is virtually impossible to capture the wonder, the beauty, the provocations at every turn in this program. Surrounded by flowers, herbs, and vegetable plants, children cross a little wooden bridge into a mysterious, relaxing, intimate outdoor enclosure, complete with rugs, pillows, sheer coverings, chimes, more plants, and baskets of books. Following a raised wooden ramp walkway from this cozy, tucked-away haven, children wind through the towering plants into the outdoor loose-parts area. Here their imaginations run wild, leading to all kinds of innovations! As engineers, they design and construct contraptions of all sorts, using a small ladder, metal crank and pipes, large- and medium-sized wooden spools, lumber stored in different-sized clay pots, tires, and wooden pallets, all placed on rubber-matted flooring. Flowing easily between the outdoors and indoors, children explore seemingly endless STEM opportunities, ranging from designing and creating at the sewing table (with needles, thread, plastic straws, burlap, beads, and ribbon) to planning and constructing at the Frank Lloyd Wright architecture center (stocked with books about the architect, protractors, colored pencils, clipboards, and a variety of blocks) to exploring patterns with tinker tray collections of loose parts (from buttons and pebbles to feathers and tiny pine cones). And did I mention the large outdoor mud area where children experiment with bottles of colored water, stirring up soup with sets of measuring cups and cooking utensils or excavating a work site using their dump trucks, buckets, and shovels?

The center's messages and values are loud and clear to visitors: all children are competent and capable (and thus can learn to sew with teacher support or build safely with large tires), all children have the right to engage in inquiry (and thus can garden or experiment with mud), and all children have the right to explore and wonder in a magical environment. All children deserve opportunities to communicate their ideas and perspectives, collaborate with others as they make plans, critically think about the rich content around them, and develop their confidence in taking risks and solving problems in an environment that includes outdoor spaces and small intimate spaces. Or, as the head teacher says, "In corners, under, and behind, they explore with wonder!"

CHAPTER 3:
THE USE OF TIME

An environment is a living changing system. More than the physical space, it includes the way time is structured.

—Lella Gandini in *The Hundred Languages of Children*, 3rd ed.

For children to fully engage in playful investigations and project-based STEM learning, they benefit from uninterrupted blocks of time stretched throughout the day, sometimes over several days or even over weeks. As stated in *STEM Learning with Young Children*, "Children's inquiry is supported by a schedule that allows ample time for children to engage with the materials . . . a sufficient length of time that allows for extended exploration, investigation, and experimentation" (Counsell et al. 2016, 37).

For example, let's say the children have indicated an interest in creating a class vegetable garden, as the Amen Nursery School did, after learning about and tasting different categories of food (fruits, vegetables, breads/grains, and so forth). There are endless STEM concepts to explore and so much rich vocabulary to acquire. The STEM learning that takes place around gardening can be astounding but clearly involves lots of time spread out over weeks. Such a study might start with questions from the children and the teachers, including the following:

- What do plants need to grow?

- Where should we plant our garden so that plants can thrive?

- Can we grow plants in pots or containers?

- What tools do we need?

- Which books, videos, and experts would be helpful resources?

- Are there gardens near our program that we can visit and explore?

- What if we don't have a place to garden?

Once we co-research our questions together, Reggio style, using our resources to gather information about planting and tending our garden, we need to make a plan that identifies materials (soil, seeds, seedlings, stakes) and gardening tools (rake, digging tools, watering can, hose), and considers how to get these items (from others' gardens, donations from local farms). Perhaps families will loan us tools or large pots and containers, and volunteers will help us dig out the garden area or build raised beds. Once we have our spot or containers prepared and the necessary materials and tools assembled, then we will plant our seeds or seedlings, labeling each one in English and perhaps other languages. Tending our garden involves many responsibilities: watering our plants, weeding, noticing beneficial and harmful insects, and watching each new stage of growth. During our garden study, there will be many wondrous observations, questions, changes, and exciting learning moments, and we will document our questions, comments, surprises, and new learning using plans, blueprints, drawings, lists, photos, and videos. While we observe, photograph, chart, and measure the plants' growth (and decay), we will learn about the life cycles of plants, worms, and insects; the importance of sunlight, soil, and water; the parts of plants; the impact of weather; and composting. Finally, with a little luck and lots of patience, we can harvest our garden, enjoy a taste-testing celebration, and share our documentation of STEM learning with families. Along the way, we will learn about eating nutritiously and organically and instill the importance of caring for our planet and all living things. We practice the 6Cs as we communicate and collaborate about our garden design and our tools, discuss rich content about plant life, create documentation, and build our confidence in using tools and caring for living things.

Of course many programs do not have an area where they can plant a garden. However, valuable STEM learning opportunities are still available with a little imagination and investigation, such as gardening in containers, visiting and studying at a community garden or family garden, or visiting a park or common space where there are plants and seasonal changes to study. During one of my study trips to Reggio Emilia, we visited a city community garden where all ages admired and observed the life cycles of vegetables, fruit, and flowers while enjoying the camaraderie. We joyfully shared an outdoor meal together, eating, singing, and dancing on the old basketball court next to the community garden and senior center.

Although a gardening study or similar investigation promotes wonder, curiosity, and important STEM learning, early childhood educators throughout the United States with whom I have worked reluctantly agree that their preschools generally have tightly structured daily schedules, making carving out flexible time for children to engage in such stretched-out STEM investigations seem too challenging. They voice their frustrations, complaining that there just isn't enough time in the day for extended studies or that their administrators or curricular expectations don't allow for such flexible time. Their days are already packed with the day-to-day "requirements." Starting with drop-off, preschool teachers need to check in with parents or caregivers while warmly greeting children, then oversee children putting away their jackets, coats, mittens, boots, hats, and backpacks. Once children are settled in, teachers then balance free play, center time, circle time, read-aloud time, outdoor play, hand washing, and snacktime, and end their day cleaning up, packing up, and sharing hugs and goodbyes. (This of course does not include emergency drills, guest visits, children getting sick, or planning and preparing!) Full-day programs also schedule lunch, brushing teeth, and naptime. Somewhere in between, teachers try to squeeze in informal or required assessments. Most of us agree that a smoothly running program requires structure and time management and that young children benefit from knowing what to expect. Thus, many teachers I know feel that finding flexible time or extended time for playful STEM studies is not realistic, doable, or supported by administrators. It is difficult to embrace a philosophical change that doesn't seem workable, despite the probable value and benefits of such change.

Given the challenges of finding flexible time to conduct a long-term STEM study, we discuss the goals of their tightly scheduled preschool program and consider if there are ways to meet them other than through their typically scheduled day, thereby creating more flexible time for playful STEM inquiry. Most often in this discussion, teachers mention developmental and curricular goals that must be met: social and emotional skills, listening, self-help and self-regulatory skills, fine- and gross-motor skills, receptive and expressive language development, early literacy, and early math. We then consider whether these goals are at least partially attainable (possibly even in much more depth) through inquiry-based STEM studies rather than always relying on organized centers, circle time, and free play. Teachers begin to consider that STEM investigations and project-based learning are most often interdisciplinary; thus, the goals of the typical schedule might also be realized through STEM studies.

I saw this in action when I visited a Boston part-day preschool program where there was lots of noisy construction taking place on the busy street outside the classrooms. Many of the children excitedly commented on this construction work as they arrived at the preschool or observed it through the classroom windows. So much to see and hear: workers in tool belts, yellow hats, and vests directing one another, signs, yellow tape, cones, big machinery, wheelbarrows, big holes in the ground, piles of materials, lots of tools. Tapping into the excitement, teachers began a class study of the construction project, starting with the children listing their observations and questions. Together they read a range of nonfiction and fiction children's books about cities, transportation, construction, types of workers, signs, tools, and machinery, and looked at blueprints and maps—all early literacy (and STEM) opportunities promoting background knowledge and vocabulary development. With frequent short walks outdoors, during all kinds of weather, they captured the construction site progress over time, bringing back to the classroom their notes and data for analysis. All along, the teachers and the children documented their outdoor and indoor learning, including their own ongoing classroom block construction site with trucks, handwritten signs, and various kinds of toy workers; journal drawings and labels for the construction site and block construction; and photos and videos of the workers using their tools and equipment. Through this interdisciplinary and integrated project-based study, children were engaged not only in the

6Cs but also in all the developmental goals and skills that preschool teachers in my course had described as essential: developing social learning, self-help and self-regulatory skills, listening, language development, early literacy, and early math. They were able to engage in this authentic STEM/interdisciplinary investigation because the teachers used time differently and flexibly, finding time for their study while still meeting the goals of the program without relying on such strict daily adherence to the schedule.

Providing extended time for STEM topics, though challenging, also benefits different kinds of learners. In their essay in the book *Environment*, De Arment, Xu, and Coleman describe the importance of the "temporal environment . . . schedules and routines as well as pacing and sequence of activities" (2016, 40). Their particular emphasis is on creating an environment that supports all learners, including those who need more time and those who need time structured differently. Some children need a slowed-down schedule with many opportunities to practice before learning begins to take place. Consider the STEM skills required in using wooden blocks to create a construction site: recognizing attributes of different blocks (size, color, shape, length, width, weight), learning about patterns (recognizing, repeating, extending, creating patterns), utilizing estimating skills (about how many more are needed to finish the building or highway bridge), and developing some beginning understanding of balance and gravity. At the same time, children use the 6Cs and practice the habits of adult scientists and engineers (designing, testing, revising, making mistakes, dealing with frustration, showing patience). For some children, particularly those with many prior experiences, much of this learning happens quickly without intentional sequencing or a lot of practice. If they need little teacher intervention and scaffolding, a limited, more tightly scheduled routine might be acceptable for them. But children of differing abilities or limited background knowledge may require more sequential, step-by-step, or extended opportunities to explore and practice, as well as time for teacher modeling and direct intervention.

Although a garden study takes extensive time and careful planning with the children and volunteers, STEM learning opportunities also arise from unplanned or incidental teachable moments. For example, if children wondered about color combinations after reading the book *Little Blue and Little Yellow* (Leonni 2017), teachers would want flexibility in the schedule to spontaneously experiment with watercolors or food coloring. Or if in reading *It Looked Like Spilt Milk* (Shaw 2014), children raised questions about clouds, the teacher would value having time to take the children outdoors and observe cloud formations. These kinds of incidental experiences may lead to more extended studies of weather or the water cycle.

Together the students in my class and I brainstormed options for finding extended blocks of time, with peers sharing their creative solutions as they experimented during the course. For example, one preschool teacher explained how she found time for a long garden study. Instead of her daily circle time and end-of-the-day read-alouds, she chose books about gardening and plants to take outside to read as the class began the day's gardening tasks. This linked the book with the STEM activity while freeing up some additional time for the study by not having two separate read-aloud times during the day. While her assistant and parent volunteer worked with children who could readily manage learning new tasks to work in one part of the garden, she worked with those who required more intentional step-by-step intervention and practice on other gardening tasks. These solutions did not create extensive amounts of flexible time, but they freed her and the children to find more precious minutes to pursue their gardening study in a way that made sense for everyone.

Self-Assessment Checklist

- Could you start your day differently? What if children arrived and immediately continued with a project started the day before rather than circle time or center time? Or what if children arrived to be surprised by a provocation or puzzling item to spur conversation, questions, and further study during the week? How could you bend the schedule for this investigation?

- Which activities or routines are really necessary? What would happen if you cut something out or reduced its time or frequency? Do you need a separate daily read-aloud at a certain time, or could it be incorporated into a STEM study?

- Which daily scheduled events are "old scripts" that can be modified to allow flexible time for "new scripts"? For example, for one week, could outdoor playtime become the outdoor classroom for a STEM study?

- Do you capture "teachable moments" and provide immediate, spontaneous incidental teaching to respond to children's urgent and curious questions? Considering the examples in this chapter, how could you alter the schedule to respond to children's questions about colors or clouds?

- Is there a more efficient way to end the day? Perhaps volunteers could assist with cleanup, share notices with families, or help children pack up their belongings to open up a little time.

- Which times of the day work best for children's engagement with STEM activities? Which times of the day work best for outdoor STEM activities?

- Is there another way to take care of school business without using class time? Can you use technology to free up time during the day? How can you more efficiently use apps, your class/school website, parent notice board, or newsletter to save a few minutes at the beginning and end of the day?

- Is there a way you can provide more time for small groups of students to pursue a topic? For example, can children interested in shadow and light inquiry continue their investigations with you while others continue with the daily schedule with the teaching assistant or volunteers (or vice versa)?

- How can you collaborate with colleagues to create a more flexible schedule? Can you team teach? Can one of you support one study while the other colleague supports another? Perhaps your group wants to study body mechanics and exercise while your colleague's group is excited to discover and document patterns found in nature and architecture.

One Thing to Try Tomorrow

Take a quick peek at your daily schedule. Try this without judgment, remembering there is no score, no right or wrong response, no evaluator looking on. Put your feet up, close your eyes, and allow yourself a moment to imagine. In your ideal world, what would you like your day and the children's day to look like? Would you like to incorporate more flexible time for an exciting STEM study? Would you like for children to have time to use their senses just to notice, wonder, enjoy? How do you think children's time should or could be spent—at least on some days, if not every day? Consider what would happen if you experimented with changing one small thing in your schedule tomorrow. What could you do a little differently or a little more flexibly? If you typically maintain the same routine every day, could something be eliminated? Could something be shortened? For some days or weeks, could outdoor playtime transform into an outdoor investigation? Is there some STEM project you'd love to do that you've never had time to do? What would excite you? Maybe you love the STEM concepts associated with music (volume, tempo, vibrations, dancing, singing) or cooking (reading recipes, measuring and mixing ingredients, cooking, freezing or baking, and tasting, of course) or creatively constructing and inventing with loose parts (jewelry, habitats, creatures, elaborate patterns, a new tool). Or maybe you've heard a child passionately asking a question about reflections when there wasn't time to investigate with mirrors. If you go in tomorrow excited about your interest or the child's interest, your wonder, curiosity, and enthusiasm will be contagious!

Just go for it—try tweaking the schedule a little bit tomorrow (or all week!), finding a little flexible time for inquiry and playful STEM investigations. Remember that working with a like-minded colleague can be supportive and also might free you both to find more flexible time. You might even try some collaborative STEM investigations, finding time to work together while also modeling the 6Cs. Reggio educators prioritize regular professional collaboration, planning together for investigations and finding ways to make them happen. Creating flexible time for playful, inquiry-based STEM investigations requires a little risk-taking, with one small step into thinking outside the box.

Snapshot: Elisabeth Amen Nursery School

Extending time for life science studies, Amen Nursery School children explore the Wheaton nature trail

As children arrive in one of the preschool classrooms, rather than starting center time or circle time right away, they are immediately invited to explore interesting and puzzling new props, such as a plastic model of a water pump similar to the real (extremely heavy) pump that is being added to the outdoor kitchen. The teacher encourages the children to start their day taking risks investigating the pump and asking questions about it as they consider its texture, design, material, purpose, operation, and how it might fit into their developing outdoor classroom. The children start the day with exploration, even if just for a few minutes, a time that might otherwise have been absorbed into their center play or circle time. As college students or parent volunteers assist with monitoring the centers and children's play, the teacher and a small group of interested children engage in further exploration of the water pump (or some other investigation). The Amen Nursery School is also fortunate to have easy access to campus nature areas. Observing ripples of water or noisy geese at the pond or walking on the nature trail through the woods provides children time to develop interest in studying the plants and animals of the ecosystems around them. Of course visiting the pond or nature trail means the teacher has decided to let something else in the schedule go, to allow for STEM investigations to surface. These choices reflect the values of the teachers and the messages they want to convey.

The director points out that staff needed time to acclimate to creating a more inquiry-based STEM outdoor learning environment. As she explains, "Teachers are familiar and comfortable with the indoor classroom. However, finding enough time to effectively learn how to thoughtfully and flexibly use the new outdoor classroom, the pond, the apple orchard, or the woods for STEM studies is challenging." While the new outdoor classroom and the pond, orchard, and woods encourage inquiry and investigation, they also require a rethinking of the schedule in different ways. Children need time to get there and back, as well as time to select and return with buckets, pails, nets, pots and pans, gardening tools, boots, and other tools. Thus, teachers not only need to be flexible and creative with time but also need to enhance their own professional skills and develop efficiency in their routines.

In the fall of 2020, in the midst of the worldwide pandemic and the cautious reopening of the nursery school, the staff had to be even more flexible in their use of time. The director asked the teachers to plan for full days in the outdoor classroom, in the woods, at the pond, and at the apple orchard (as well as indoors in poor weather). As the teachers rose to the challenge and gained familiarity with the other outdoor resources, many interesting STEM studies could flourish in these environments with this revised scheduling and use of time.

Snapshot: Local Head Start Program

The Head Start teacher brought branches into the classroom as a provocation during their study of trees. These natural learning materials cost nothing and supported children's hands-on sensory learning about trees while providing time for more open-ended playful exploration.

Believing in the competency of children, the Head Start teacher allowed the children to practice hammering nails into the wooden workbench (under supervision). Next the children put nails into the ends of the stripped down, smooth branches during the tree study and tested out the embedded nails in experiments with magnets.

The Head Start federally required curriculum encourages an incremental, step-by-step approach to learning that relies on a structured schedule. Units of study incorporate a sequence of lessons that teachers implement within their settings. While the teachers agree that sequential learning is important, they also consider opportunities for more playful explorations valuable but struggle to find flexible time. To balance the structured curriculum with more playful investigations, the staff modifies the schedule in a variety of ways. For example, the teachers regularly work at tables with small groups on the required STEM study while other children are provided a range of theme-related choices to investigate independently. Alternating these groups allows each child to benefit from both experiences: working with their teacher on the more structured curriculum and engaging in more open-ended exploration. While a teacher meets with a small group of children during the tree study, other children choose between creating tree rubbings and working with tree shavings. College students often volunteer, monitoring children's playful explorations while listening to and capturing their comments and questions. While one teacher and her children are reading a book on transportation, other children are using blocks to build roads, bridges, and airports for their cars, trucks, buses, and planes. These alternating experiences also allow children to practice the 6Cs as they collaboratively and creatively design their constructions.

Inviting an "expert" on the topic of study is another effective strategy. It requires either letting something else go for part of the day or having the expert work with just a small group of interested children while the others continue with their typical schedule. The director urges her staff to "Be creative! You can find someone! And you can find the time!" For example, when the children were studying clothing followed by a study of exercise and body mechanics, the director became the "expert" and surprised them with her karate outfit and kicks while reinforcing both topics. Although this did not provide for an extended, complex opportunity for study over several days or weeks, arranging the schedule to make room for the "expert" deepened children's discussion of the topic and conveyed how the teachers value having more flexible time. Walking field trips to the nearby fire and police stations, library, and college campus also initiate or extend a topic of study. These excursions require a willingness to depart from the typical daily schedule in favor of expanding these STEM studies. Planting seeds in pots to take home and caring for them with their families allowed children to extend time on their own personalized investigations. They were encouraged to share their results with the class, bringing their plant back into the classroom or showing photos or drawings. By creatively extending time on these topics, teachers are also sharing the values of respect for life, nature, and sustainability.

These busy Head Start teachers, who are accountable to strict federal guidelines, struggle to find sufficient time for much-needed STEM professional development. Using the program app GOLD Documentation by Teaching Strategies, they have found online STEM curricular resources including children's books, songs, photos, key vocabulary related to a particular study, and more. This resource saves them professional time building background knowledge, searching for ideas, planning, and preparing materials.

Snapshot: Anchorage Park Kindergarten

The head teacher describes the use of time as both a philosophical and a leadership question. She states, "It's essential to have time to connect with the child. . . . Time is a matter of how children see us. That is, if a child wants your time, they are entitled to that time—for help, support, advice, or celebration. What's more important?" An essential aspect of time is "recognizing, responding to, and capturing the moments to celebrate the wonder, excitement, and learning of the children." Of course, as with any program, there are boundaries, routines, and expectations, but as she strongly argues, "If children's time isn't valuable, then why are we here?" There is no compulsory component to the day in her program (as in some programs, such as Head Start), so giving children the time they need "honors them." She explains that her center has a rolling tea (or what we in the United States would call snacktime). If a child is hungry at tea time, that is great. But if they come to school hungry or get hungry later in the day after tea, she argues, "Why should they have to wait two hours to eat? That's a basic right of children." Adjusting to the changing nature of groups in the center also requires a fluid sense of time. For example, at one time they had more three-year-olds in the program than four- and five-year-olds. Their "brains and bodies are not in a box. We have to consider how to use our time to work with this younger group." She notes that as the children mature, they adjust to program restrictions. She also speaks of children with additional learning needs: "It is our responsibility to honor them, to adjust our program and time with them accordingly."

CHAPTER 4:
THE USE OF SPACE

Educators in Reggio Emilia speak of space as a "container" that favors social interaction, exploration, and learning, but they also see space as having educational "content."

—Lella Gandini citing Tiziana Filippini's observations in *The Hundred Languages of Children*, 3rd ed.

In *The Hundred Languages of Children* (2012, 320), Lella Gandini describes the intentional design of space, or what she refers to as the "container"—a laboratory that holds adults and children engaged in learning together. In designing this nurturing container, the educators ensure that the space reflects their values and messages (as discussed in chapter 2). A value of great importance is the creation of a "relational space." In a relational space, teachers nurture an inclusive culture of child and adult communication and collaboration where all children have access to playful learning opportunities. Gender, race, ethnicity, religion, and first languages are respected, and the space also values universal design, whereby all children can access learning experiences. Some children require accommodations such as high-contrast visual aids, slant boards, lap trays, touch screens, seating devices, or widened areas that allow walkers and wheelchairs to maneuver. Additionally, all children deserve and require multisensory learning opportunities, multiple means of expression, and varied opportunities to show what they know. This inclusive culture values the contributions that all children bring to the space.

Relationships evolve as children and adults practice careful listening, expressing their ideas and respecting differing perspectives, all of which are important to STEM studies. For example, a study of sound might begin with a discussion of children's favorite songs or their experience with various instruments. As children discuss their preferences, teachers listen for teachable moments or incidental learning opportunities to pursue further study. This carefully designed relational space mirrors the environments in which STEM professionals, such as medical researchers or engineers, conduct their work: in teams, communicating and sharing insights from diverse perspectives. As Susan Stacey states in her book *Inquiry-Based Early Learning Environments* (2019), "We can think of it as a space that intrigues us to move in new directions and as a setting where relationships are formed, decisions are made, and a particular culture—a way of being—might be formed" (2). This relational space conveys the importance of collaborative work, communication, creativity, critical thinking, rich content, and confidence building.

The design and use of the space also reflects Reggio teachers' respect for children's competencies and capabilities. For example, materials are carefully selected and placed in the space in intriguing ways to invite wonder, curiosity, bewilderment, and surprise. Thoughtfully chosen materials provide provocations to spur STEM explorations. Surprising and enticing materials invite children's sensory exploration, examining properties such as texture, weight, and shape while promoting creativity and innovation. Materials may be natural or machine made, placed indoors or out, to capture children's imaginations and springboard STEM studies. Some provocative items and materials also surprise (and sometimes concern) many US preschool teachers, who worry about safe handling and usage. After initial instruction, Reggio children are typically trusted to responsibly use sharp tools or breakable items. For example, in the classic video *To Make a Portrait of a Lion* (Malaguzzi [1987] 2015), Reggio children use the outdoor piazza space to touch, climb on, photograph, and measure a lion statue and its shadow. Then, in their indoor space, they continue and expand their study of lions. Children use pointed artist's tools to add details to their sophisticated clay lion sculptures. Nearly every time I have shown this video to preschool teachers, alarmed facial expressions and verbal comments convey their concerns that these tools are unsafe or developmentally inappropriate for preschoolers (not to mention their climbing on the lion statue, which was much taller than the children). But for Reggio educators, young children are considered capable of using such artist's tools and materials once properly introduced.

In the Reggio-inspired space, furniture is carefully chosen to support children's learning. During my visits, I observed the various qualities of furniture: comfort, durability, weight, and pleasing colors. The furniture was also selected for easy reconfiguration, to accommodate the space for group work and changing group sizes, as well as for children who use wheelchairs, walkers, or other adaptive equipment. Easily movable furniture allows children to push their chairs together for more intimate discussions and work or arrange chairs for whole-class sharing. Movable furniture creates interim open spaces for large and extended investigations, such as building projects with blocks or a series of ramps for experiments with balls and toy cars, allowing these projects to evolve from simple, short-term activities into more complex and challenging studies, remaining in place for days or even weeks. In US classrooms, such investigations are often cut short, with no dedicated area (or time) for extended and deep study, reflection, and documentation, as the limited space is needed for other activities. Most often, children need to take apart their constructions and put them away at the end of the day. To promote investigations, Gandini (2012) notes that, similar to time, the space needs to be flexible and adaptable.

Unfortunately, the teachers with whom I have worked are often discouraged and frustrated by the limitations of space in their settings. Preschools in the United States are housed in a wide variety of settings, including church basements, shopping plazas, large child care centers and chains, family homes, Head Start settings, college settings, public schools, and corporations. Many preschools in the United States are located in inflexible, inappropriate old containers. For example, I worked for several years in two early childhood programs, one housed in a wing of an old high school and the other in the former middle school home economics classroom, with neither space designed for young children's learning. Some of the furniture consisted of leftovers from unused classrooms.

Clutter is also a hallmark of many US classrooms. Well-intended teachers (myself included!) love yard sales where we find low-cost materials we think we will use at some point. And we are famous for enthusiastically saying yes when family and friends get rid of children's books, games, and art supplies. Given our efforts to reuse and recycle an endless array of possible learning materials, we often end up piling them on classroom windowsills and counters, cramming them into shelves, and stuffing them into closets (if we even have closets). Often these materials remain unused because they are buried under other materials, out of reach for both adults and children. Teachers can review their space in light of the values and messages they want to convey and begin to intentionally cull their materials, reorganize them, and store selected materials in ways that create a more pleasing sense of order for both children and adults. In this way, precious space is freed for photo panels, collections of shells, beads, and pebbles, or an observation station for bird studies. Eye-pleasing baskets and wooden boxes enhance organization, storage, and visibility. Moving materials into clear, labeled bins provides for easier accessibility, respecting the capabilities of children to access and return materials or tools they use in their investigations.

To create more flexible space, teachers in Reggio Emilia embrace the outdoor areas around their schools. This includes the immediate outdoors as well as the nearby neighborhood and the broader community, whether it is urban, suburban, or rural. For example, children in the city can search for architectural patterns in sidewalks, windows, doors, fences, and railings. Children can paint the patterns they observe at an outdoor easel, build a sidewalk or wall with blocks and stones, or take digital photos to document their observations. Children in a more rural area can follow a path across a field, spreading their collected treasures on a blanket to admire, discuss, sort, identify, compare and contrast, document, and eventually exhibit in a class museum. Children in a suburban area can plant seeds in the school or community garden, tend the plants, weed the garden, pick the vegetables as they grow, observe the worms, bees, and butterflies, and notice how the vegetables decay, documenting their investigations with digital photos, drawings, and stories. Their world becomes a classroom space.

Working with preschool teachers from a wide range of settings, I have observed how they often find creative solutions to expand limited indoor classroom space, particularly for STEM investigations that require room for groups of children to work with a lot of materials spread out over several days. Some have taken a close look at their furniture, noting what is useful and what is not. Amen School volunteers built lofts in each classroom for small-group collaboration or reflection. Other teachers have teamed with colleagues to share two classrooms. As they reimagine their settings, the teachers need to agree on their priorities, values, and messages, as discussed in chapter 2. Collaboration allows for negotiating what is essential and what might be considered an "old script" as the current use of space no longer reflects their evolving philosophies. Perhaps they agree that one room will be designated for a more stationary arrangement of traditional centers while the other room supports more dynamic, open-ended investigations. Other teachers have shared how they have negotiated their indoor spaces to include (at least some of the time) stairwells, hallways, infrequently used office space, and sporadically used common space in the building. In fact, one Reggio program I visited converted an unused attic space that had previously collected dusty materials into a living, breathing neighborhood museum to exhibit treasured artifacts discovered and donated by families.

Reggio educators value the integration of the indoor space with the outdoor space. Children look through windows to study birds at the bird feeder or watch changing weather patterns. Natural items from the outdoors are brought indoors for observation and study. Conversely, the outdoors is viewed as an extended space for learning, particularly inspiring for STEM studies on topics like the life cycles of plants and animals, the water cycle, cloud formations, wind, and states of matter, such as icicles and melting snow. However, despite teachers' desires, many preschools in the United States have limited options for outdoor learning spaces. For example, in one inner-city program that I supervised, the playground had to be cleared each morning of unsanitary and sometimes dangerous debris left by nighttime adult intruders who hung out there. Creative teachers (including those in the Snapshots) have shared strategies for creating extended outdoor learning spaces. Parking areas can be used between drop-off and pickup (with safety features such as cones in place) for investigations like shadow studies. Other preschool teachers expand their space with regular small-group or class walks to a nearby woods, pond, park, college, or public space to study architecture, trees, or types of transportation. These options can be time consuming to arrange and require thoughtful planning, but generally they are doable, often by collaborating with colleagues, parents, volunteers, or college students. Accessing outdoor learning spaces involves planning for and accommodating all children's successful experiences, including those who require wheelchairs, walkers, one-to-one behavior monitoring, and visual or hearing accommodations.

Using outdoor spaces for playful STEM investigation reflects the values of the teacher by fostering children's appreciation for the living world and the web of life. Observing and documenting frogs, turtles, fish, worms, bees, spiderwebs, streams, wildflowers, twigs, pine cones, and leaves allows children to experience, feel, and savor wonder. Reggio teachers speak passionately about children's rights. I would argue that wonder is a child's right. Indoor and outdoor spaces where children experience wonder nurture their developing appreciation and sense of responsibility toward taking care of our planet.

Self-Assessment Checklist

- Consider the value of videotaping your indoor and outdoor space for reflection or to document change over time.

- Do the opportunities provided by your space range in levels of complexity, providing for those who need more teacher intervention and practice as well as for those who are ready for more challenging experiences?

- Is your space too cluttered? Are books stuffed in shelves? Are containers of materials piled sky high? Is your closet overflowing? If so, how might you declutter your space? What do you really need? What can you give away to colleagues and families? How can you organize and store materials for easy access for adults and children?

- How can you design your space so that children with mobility challenges and children with wheelchairs or specialized adaptive equipment feel safe and engaged, and have a sense of belonging?

- Do you maximize the use of your space? Have you considered varying the use of the shelving, furniture, windows and windowsills, walls, floor, lofts, intimate spaces, hallway, and stairwell?

- How might you collaborate with colleagues to use shared spaces more flexibly?

- How do you bring the outdoors in? Do you need curtains or shades? Do you need tinted windows? Where might you set up observation stations with binoculars, recording materials (paper, pens, cameras, and so forth) and nonfiction books for studying birds, weather, changing seasons, and so forth?

- Is your space comfortable? Are there soft, movable items for sitting and collaborating? Are there intimate spaces for quiet, reflective work? How might you use a loft or divider?

- What materials do you need to make regular use of the outdoor space easier? Do you need rain boots, umbrellas, rain jackets, or gloves organized and ready to go for each child, yourself, and volunteers/assistants? Do you have STEM tools ready to go: buckets, clipboards, digital cameras or tablets, magnifying glasses, binoculars, tweezers, shovels, nets? Do you need large umbrellas or tarps to protect yourselves from the sun or rain?

- How do you maximize outdoor opportunities for STEM learning: a nearby stream, birdhouses and feeders, gardens, shadow play on the sidewalk, puddle play, bridge building, tree studies, mud kitchens?

- Do you model and emphasize the importance of recycling, reducing, and reusing in your space? Do you model respect and responsible care for your natural environment?

One Thing to Try Tomorrow

Revisit that video you took after reading chapter 2 (that's the power of documentation: the opportunity to revisit and reflect!). If you decided not to brave the video (or didn't read chapter 2), take a few minutes now to take out your phone or tablet and slowly pan your setting (both indoors and outdoors). Even better, do it with a like-minded and nonjudgmental colleague. (At the least, you'll share the misery, or you may even have a few laughs!) Remember, this is not a test. Review your video together, asking, "Does my setting provide an inclusive space for playful STEM investigations that could take place over a few days or a week?" If not, don't give up! Ask yourself and your colleague what one small thing you could change that would get the ball rolling to support your evolving philosophy about the importance of space in the playful, inquiry-based STEM environment. One of the many goals for this book is to emphasize the availability and usefulness of no-cost or low-cost ways to promote playful STEM literacy, so I'm not suggesting that you advocate for all-new materials or new furniture as described above. Take a walk in your building. What about the hallway? A colleague's office that seldom gets used? What about a stairwell (where I once saw Reggio children working on a project that involved inclines)? Take a walk outside. Is there a place to start a garden or grow container plants? Is there a place for an outdoor kitchen, perhaps starting with a water table with some pots and pans? Could you use the sidewalk or parking area for shadow studies or for experiments with balls and ramps? How about the surrounding neighborhood? What is nearby that you could take advantage of? When you hit those yard sales and receive donations, keep your philosophy in mind. First, remember the clutter and choose wisely! Then keep an eye out for useful chairs and tables for your setting or some nonfiction science or nature books. Perhaps you will find clear bins or baskets for storage or a shelving unit you could place in the hallway outside your classroom. Good yard sales often include collections of shells, rocks, balls, marbles, magnets, toy cars and figures, blocks, magnifying glasses, tweezers, tubes, funnels, fabrics, nuts, bolts, screws, and all kinds of loose parts you could carefully and intentionally select for your STEM space.

Might your like-minded, nonjudgmental colleague be willing to team up with you to create a flexible space for STEM investigations (as well as other worthy projects)? It's easy when considering space to become overwhelmed or frustrated and say, "Never mind!" But taking your time and starting small, building success step-by-step, makes lofty goals seem within reach—not to mention satisfying and fulfilling.

Snapshot: Elisabeth Amen Nursery School

Changes to the Amen Nursery School environment have not happened overnight and are ever in progress. They began some time ago when the former director and I traveled to Reggio Emilia as part of a small study group. The former director was so inspired by the early childhood environments she encountered in Reggio that she began to work with her staff on small steps they could take to create a more inviting learning environment. Her first project was reevaluating and transforming the entrance hallway (or what would mirror in spirit a small piazza in Reggio Emilia). She invited a volunteer who was an art student to paint an inviting trail of ivy throughout the entrance hallway where examples of children's work began to appear. Considering the importance of integrating indoor and outdoor spaces, she had the massive picture windows in each setting tinted so that children could observe the newly installed bird feeders and the changing weather without direct sunlight in their eyes. Always an advocate for a playful emergent curriculum based on children's interests, she and her staff began to emphasize inquiry-based STEM opportunities, beginning with the children and families planting an outdoor garden.

STEM opportunities are integrated throughout the indoor and outdoor classrooms for children to actively and collaboratively investigate, invent, construct, research, and reflect. According to the new director, "Spaces take into consideration all types of children. Some don't want to sit [for] a long time, some need to rehash, and some need a place to calm down or regroup. Respecting the child is where it starts when creating the environment in this space."

The director told a story showing the benefits of the new outdoor space for the 6Cs and playful STEM problem solving. In the outdoor kitchen, children figure out how to get water from the pump to the kitchen and dump the water from the heavy bucket. A preschool girl, noted for seldom asking for help, attempted to fill her bucket with water to carry to the outdoor kitchen. However, through trial and error, she discovered that the bucket was too heavy for her to manage alone. She had to ask a friend for help! Together they lugged the heavy bucket to the kitchen without spilling too much. Together they hoisted the bucket, tipped it, and poured the water into the sink. Success! As the director explained, "For this little girl, this was a big deal!" In this outdoor space (and without teacher intervention), the teachers observed the little girl using a multitude of scientific processes: grappling with a problem, testing her solutions, getting frustrated, critically considering her options, communicating with a friend, and collaborating to solve the problem.

Snapshot: Local Head Start Program

With the added greenhouse space, Head Start children were able to conduct life cycle studies planting their own seeds, tending their seedlings, and observing growth of their plants over time.

The director of this Head Start program acknowledges that, as is true for many preschools in the United States, "space is a challenge for us. Every room is different and each teacher has a different style. We consider if the space is overly stimulating while at the same time worry about meeting regulations and fire codes. We also need to consider how to organize materials for limited storage and sharing across classrooms." Despite these common challenges, this director notes that after two years of study, "STEM isn't marginalized—it is all around—even in dramatic play in these busy classrooms." Children explore the physical properties of liquids at the water table with funnels, tubes, gutters, and measuring cups, or they construct with nearby magnetic tiles.

As with the Reggio schools, Head Start teachers embrace opportunities to partner with families and use community resources. For example, with the help of local Eagle Scouts and parent volunteers, they converted a tight outdoor space to a more inviting setting by adding raised beds, a bench, and a greenhouse with plantings. Visiting the farm on the college campus extends their gardening study. Recently, the teachers struggled to find space to exhibit children's work for an end-of-the-study celebration. Using spray-painted recycled and repurposed boxes, they transformed the cramped entrance hallway into a museum where children, families, and staff mingled and admired the children's work.

Snapshot: Anchorage Park Kindergarten

In the relatively big and open spaces at Anchorage Park Kindergarten, constructions can be left in place for children's extended explorations over time.

The head teacher views the use of space philosophically, asking the provocative question, "Who owns the space?" Decisions are made by "looking at space from a child's eye"—considering the competencies of children, exploring how children learn, recognizing what children need, asking what makes sense and what will support children in learning responsibility and respect. The staff considers how they work with children individually, in small groups, and with their families, exploring such questions as, "How will the space be used?" "How do children fit?" "How do adults fit?" "What could we move?" "What's around the corner?" "What would be soft and comfortable?"

Some outdoor spaces are relatively big and open, allowing for STEM investigations with tires, lumber, and old tractor parts. When their projects call for even larger areas, teachers consider how the nearby school hall, designated for special community events, can be temporarily converted to meet their needs, such as when they celebrated family disco night. Working together, the families, children, and staff moved furniture and materials to make way for lights, disco balls, and streamers. Because the children helped to transform the space, they were excited that the space was still theirs yet also different. On other occasions, the center has become an art gallery displaying children's work. Nearby, the school driveway has become the site of racing events. The staff continues to tweak their use of space, always mindful of their core philosophy of respecting the competencies of children.

CHAPTER 5: AESTHETICS

Reggio educators in recent years have been communicating in ever stronger ways their commitment to the aesthetic values of beauty, harmony, and order, as a way of knowing for children.

—Carolyn Edwards, Lella Gandini, and George Forman in *The Hundred Languages of Children*, 3rd ed.

Creating beautiful, harmonious spaces filled with materials that appeal to the senses is integral to the Reggio philosophy. The value that Reggio educators place on space correlates with how they value aesthetics. That is, the harmonious and aesthetically pleasing environment reflects the intentional arrangement of the room and the careful choice and arrangement of materials and furniture. Reggio classrooms invite curiosity with their emphasis on natural materials (wood, clay, grasses, feathers, stones) that are intentionally arranged and ordered to heighten their visual appeal and provoke children's wonder. Children's sensory explorations of materials through touch, smell, vision, hearing, and taste (when appropriate) are important to early STEM learning, and from my experience, the Reggio appeal to aesthetics provides a rich sensory palette, enticing children to engage in STEM learning.

Walking into such a classroom, children might find an array of beautiful seashells arranged from tiny ones to large conch shells. Observing them closely, picking them up, turning them all around, viewing them from different perspectives, holding them to their ears, and smelling them raises lots of comments and questions. Where do these come from? Are they alive? Did something live in this shell? Is this the tiniest or largest shell in the world? How did it get its shape? Why does it smell? From these questions, the children and teachers agree on a line of investigation.

Opportunities to integrate aesthetics and the senses abound in nature. For example, in the fall, the Elisabeth Amen Nursery School, like many New England preschools, typically engages children in an apple study. This complex study, evolving over weeks, begins with the children taking walks to the nearby apple orchard (which becomes an outdoor classroom on those autumn days). Along the way, the children use their senses to explore the signs of fall, observing the bright colors of the changing leaves, listening to the fallen, dry leaves crunch under their feet as they walk along, and feeling the coolness of crisp autumn air. At the apple orchard, as children admire the beauty of the orchard, they also observe growth of the apples over time. Children choose their favorite apple to pick, then feel the smooth, waxy skin, the prickly stem, and any bumps or bruises on the apple. Taking the collected apples back to the classroom, they investigate them further, comparing and contrasting the colors and sizes of the apples. Another day, they cut open the apples with the teacher, observe the core, and take out the seeds. They smell and taste the apples, describing their aroma, flavor, and crispness. They investigate red, yellow, and green apples, comparing and contrasting their attributes, likes, and dislikes. Finally, they cook applesauce with the teacher, enjoying another tasting feast. Throughout the sequence of events, the teachers (and children) document this extravaganza of the senses and STEM investigation with photos, children's drawings, new vocabulary, graphs, and children's questions and comments. During this process, children are building critical-thinking skills as they compare and contrast different tastes. Additionally, they are developing math skills as they estimate measurements and temperatures for heating and cooling and follow the sequence of steps in a recipe.

Preschool children in the United States are often unintentionally bombarded with uninviting materials or cluttered classrooms, and opportunities for STEM provocation and focus are lost. Materials stuffed in shelves or piled on the windowsill are not arranged aesthetically to invite curiosity. Many programs are filled with plastic materials, which are durable and easily cleaned but do not have the same appeal to the senses as natural materials. Working with my class of teachers, we discuss the challenge and importance of creating an appealing and inviting learning environment that aims to provoke STEM studies. Materials are chosen carefully and intentionally to spur children's curiosity and encourage them to wonder about possibilities, as well as prompt investigations and problem solving (as discussed in chapter 4, regarding space).

The Anchorage Park Kindergarten has created a truly magical environment where children are sparked to be creative and inventive risk-takers, particularly as they pursue STEM investigations. Important in their indoor and outdoor settings are tinker trays. These shallow wooden trays, aesthetically appealing to the eye, feature simple sections to order materials (most often natural materials). Purchased tinker trays are often star-shaped or rectangular with dividers, but they can just as easily be made from muffin pans, egg cartons, or similar items. The great thing about aesthetically appealing tinker trays is that what initially looks simple to engage with (counting, sorting, patterning) also allows for more complex challenges (creating, constructing, and inventing).

Self-Assessment Checklist

- When you look at your setting, do you feel a sense of beauty and order? Do you find it satisfying to look at? Is your curiosity piqued? Is it cluttered? What bothers you most?

- Is there a sense of order and harmony to the arrangement of your materials so they are visually inviting and accessible?

- How do you appeal to the children's senses? Are many of your materials made of natural elements such as wood, stone, cotton, woven grasses, or water?

- Do your windows open? How can you provide fresh air?

- Is natural light pervasive throughout your setting? If not, how might you increase it? If there is too much, how might you reduce the brightness? Do you need to tint the windows or use solar shades or curtains?

One Thing to Try Tomorrow

Thinking about the aesthetics of your setting might seem impossible with all that you have to do and the limitations of your setting in terms of materials, natural lighting, and so on. But remember, it doesn't have to be that way! Taking one small step to make your setting more aesthetically pleasing benefits children's experiences and most likely will add some surprising peace and joy to your hectic day. When you can start the day with a sense of order and harmony, you can be more mindful of children's comments, questions, and observations. If they can start the day in an aesthetically inviting setting, their wonder and curiosity and excitement for learning will be piqued—a win-win for you and your children. I have seen that many teachers with whom I work find this the most challenging change to make but also the most rewarding. So, take a deep breath (with that supportive colleague), scan your setting, and immediately describe it in one word. Did you say magical, wondrous, intriguing, *or* joyful? *Or did you say* cluttered, unorganized, busy, *or* uninviting? *No doubt there is ample evidence of what is considered essential or required curriculum, but at the same time, is there evidence of natural or beautiful materials to arouse children's senses and stimulate their curiosity? If not, consider one natural item that you could introduce into the setting tomorrow or this week. How inviting to the senses it would be to bring in some fresh herbs—lavender, mint, lemon balm, rosemary, or basil—for children to observe, smell, and feel (and maybe taste). Arranging these herbs in an appealing way in vases, mason jars, glass dishes, or pretty pots invites interest, conversation, and possibly further discussion of growing herb gardens, drying herbs, cooking with herbs, and creating items such as sachets with herbs. Most likely, a family, friend, or colleague could share some of their plants, or a nursery may be willing to donate a few small plants or seed packets so you and the children can even start your own beautiful herb garden.*

Snapshot: Elisabeth Amen Nursery School

Seated around the new table, constructed from natural materials, the children discuss investigations in their new outdoor classroom. Engaged in the 6Cs, they tinker with various tools, considering their use.

The director and staff acknowledge that their appreciation for aesthetics is primarily reflected in the beauty of nature as can be seen in their new outdoor classroom, tree and pond studies, visits to the apple orchard, and investigations into the nearby "magical woods." But as time allows, they are beginning to question the aesthetics of their indoor classrooms. The director notes emerging and important questions such as these:

- Are we stereotyping with our color choices? Should we use more neutral colors?

- How can we include more natural items such as baskets, straw mats, or wooden trays?

- What other materials could we introduce into the classroom—pebbles, feathers, shells, glass beads?

- How could we store our materials in a more enticing way and for easier access?

- How could each child's cubby become a more inviting and intimate space?

Of most concern is her insightful questioning regarding stereotyping in STEM. Many members of society devalue STEM literacy and its importance in everyday life. We often make assumptions about who is interested in STEM, who is competent in STEM areas, and who we encourage to pursue STEM careers. That is why a goal of this book, in keeping with the Reggio philosophy, is to view all children as capable and competent and to advocate that all children, regardless of gender, race, ability, socioeconomic status, first language, or religion, deserve wondrous STEM learning environments with teachers who provide opportunities for children to pursue STEM investigations.

Snapshot: Local Head Start Program

While proudly acknowledging incremental changes that have occurred in the STEM environment over the past few years, the director states that creating a more aesthetically inviting setting is challenging. Aesthetic experiences are mostly introduced incidentally through the required topics of study. For example, during the study of clothing, teachers and parents brought in different fabrics, reflecting different cultures, so that children could notice the colors, textures, and patterns and try wrapping the cloth around themselves. The children admire the natural beauty of the woods during their walks on the nearby campus nature trail, and they admire, touch, and smell the plantings in the newly constructed greenhouse. Occasional opportunities arise to engage the senses when guests play the violin or local dancers visit.

The setting is filled with materials intentionally purchased to meet curricular requirements and regulations but not chosen for their sensory or aesthetic appeal. Finding inviting and appealing ways to arrange materials is challenging, notes the director. Storage is tight and teachers must share limited resources. One small step this program has taken is to thematically group items in clearly labeled transparent storage bins. This allows children and staff to know what goes where and easily access materials. A professional development workshop, arranged by the director and facilitated by me, focused on the aesthetically inviting early childhood learning environments in Reggio Emilia and the Anchorage Park Kindergarten in Aotearoa New Zealand. During these sessions, we discuss photos of these pleasing settings, hoping that these serve as "provocations" for the staff to consider in the aesthetics of their own STEM learning environments.

Snapshot: Anchorage Park Kindergarten

Recalling the reenvisioning of their center a few years ago, the head teacher notes, "Our goal was to create an environment that children would find magical and wondrous, where they could ask questions and make connections. . . . A place where children would feel joy, not stress and anxiety." The teachers' desire to promote curiosity and inquiry contributed to the development of the aesthetic quality of the environment. Natural loose parts, such as shells, feathers, stones, and seeds, tucked away throughout the site encourage children's sorting, patterning, and creative inventions. Baskets of blocks and props, indoors and outside, support children's imaginatively engineered constructions. An outdoor easel invites children to paint or draw their impressions of flowers, trees, and clouds. Gardens foster children's understanding of life cycles and the natural world. Visiting early childhood educators from around the world (including myself) are inspired by the incredible beauty and serenity of the setting where children playfully investigate, create, and collaborate with one another and their families.

Despite these successful efforts, the head teacher also explains that environmental/climate changes continue to occur that require children and staff to adapt. Hot temperatures in recent years have dramatically challenged the natural beauty of their environment, affecting the growth of their plants. In keeping with their philosophy to respond to children's observations and to model care for our planet, the staff allowed the children to "plant" artificial flowers to maintain the beauty of their outdoor space and reduce water usage.

CHAPTER 6: MATERIALS AND THEMES

The materials should be rich and varied. They should create a multisensory setting . . . which changes over a period of time (wood, stone, flowers, fabrics) or remain unchanged (glass, steel).

—Italian architect Michele Zini, quoted in *The Hundred Languages of Children*, 3rd ed.

Carefully chosen materials invite children's curiosity, wonder, questions, puzzlement, manipulation, careful observation, conversation, and sensory exploration. All children—regardless of their classroom setting, gender, race, ethnicity, culture, religion, abilities, or socioeconomic status—deserve these opportunities derived from intentionally chosen materials. These experiences, promoting playful STEM inquiry and engagement with the scientific processes, are foundational to developing early STEM concepts.

What STEM materials are useful both indoors and outdoors? Are there loose parts for constructing and deconstructing, water and sensory tables, pots and pans, a gardening area, structures for make-believe STEM play (houses for hospitals or fire stations, tents for outdoor adventures), big blocks and tires for building structures? Not always considered a material but essential to each STEM subject area are books, both nonfiction and fiction, for children and sometimes adults. Books also help expand children's early literacy skills, building background knowledge and vocabulary.

The following sections represent possible STEM themes and materials that provoke and support investigations according to children's curiosity and interests.

Science: Discover with Balls and Ramps!

According to Betty Zan's introduction in *STEM Learning with Young Children*, science is "knowledge about or study of the natural world based on facts learned through experiments and observation" (Counsell et al. 2016, 1). In the same book, Lawrence Escalada shares that scientific processes or inquiry are integral to STEM exploration. He identifies the scientific processes as observation, communication, estimation, measurement, data collection, classification, inference, prediction, modeling, data interpretation, hypothesis, controlling variables, and defining operationally. Giving children opportunities to play with inexpensive, everyday objects encourages them to use these processes to make discoveries about their physical world. In fact, many twenty-first-century companies look for employees who can similarly play with new ideas, use their imaginations, think outside the box, take risks, and make mistakes. Additionally, employers look for employees who exhibit the 6Cs, playfully confident as they grapple with others over a design challenge. In this same playful manner, children can experiment with speed, trajectory, friction, weight, momentum, and other concepts as they design ramps and tube structures for toy cars, balls, and marbles alongside their peers. Some materials to collect and set out for STEM investigations about balls and ramps include the following:

- boards, planks, pieces of stiff cardboard, gutters, cove molding (to create ramps)

- paper towel and toilet paper tubes

- masking and duct tape (to connect components)

- various textures such as carpet pieces, sandpaper, tile, and so on (add to ramps to affect speed of balls or cars)

- small balls of all sizes and materials (foam, tennis, ping-pong, rubber, plastic)

- marbles of different sizes

- wooden spools, wooden cubes

- miniature cars

- naturally round items such as acorns, walnuts, and lemons

Of course thoughtfully chosen materials alone do not ensure learning. The teacher plays an important role (see chapter 7) scaffolding learning as children investigate the materials and concepts associated with the ramp experiments: responding to children's questions and misconceptions, asking prodding questions, facilitating more complex investigations, modeling dispositions of curiosity and risk-taking, and using and explaining content-rich vocabulary such as *motion*, *speed*, *friction*, *distance*, and *momentum*.

Technology: Test It Out!

In the December 2019 issue of *Innovations in Early Education: The International Reggio Emilia Exchange*, Brenda Fyfe reflects that Reggio educators have always incorporated technology for collaborative investigations with children, including "computers, programming software, scanners, digital cameras, video projectors, web cams, and pen microscope/cameras" (39). As we all have experienced, digital photography is integral to teaching and learning, capturing the sequence of events over time during an investigation, documenting the trials and errors experienced by the children, and displaying the scientific processes at work during the study, while also providing opportunities for children, teachers, families, and the community to revisit investigations and to celebrate their learning.

A good guideline for preschool teachers is to consider how active and engaged the children are when using technology such as tablets, computers, and smartphones. Recognizing possible negative effects of overuse of technology, organizations such as the Children's Screen Time Action Network (https://screentimenetwork.org) and TRUCE: Teachers Resisting Unhealthy Children's Entertainment (truceteachers.org) advocate for close monitoring of the amount of time preschool children spend with screens with the hope that they engage in more playful and active collaborative learning. In discussing the appropriate use of technology, Chip Donohue and Roberta Schomberg (2017) note in *Young Children*, "Technology use should not displace or replace imaginative play, outdoor play and nature, creativity, curiosity and wonder, solitary and shared experiences, or using tools for inquiry, problem solving, and exploring the world." During the pandemic, children and teachers relied on technology to stay connected to schooling. How this will ultimately play out in regard to children's overall development won't be known for some time. In the meantime, I continue to stress the intentional use of technology as discussed here.

Most often we think of technology as computers, tablets, or cell phones. However, with young children, technology is more often about problem solving and finding solutions in playful investigations, such as, "How can I keep my cow in the barnyard?" or "How can I get the heavy truck over the rickety bridge?" When discussing the appropriate use of technology in early childhood settings, I suggest that teachers give young children opportunities to freely and safely explore, handle, and test nearly everything in their environment! Push-button toys with switches and controls and more than one purpose encourage problem solving. Technological media for young children include tools such as markers, crayons, playdough, paints, pipe cleaners, and clay. Technology learning is often practiced and communicated through make-believe play, such as using the cash register, taking an X-ray, calling on the phone, setting the alarm, and mixing batter to make cookies. Here are some additional materials for exploring technology:

- make-believe play items (old cell phones, TV remotes, clocks, calculators)

- toys that promote problem solving (push buttons, switches, crank handles, flashlights, keys and locks)

Engineering: Tinker with It!

In *Engaging Young Engineers* (Stone-MacDonald et al. 2015), the authors define the engineering design process as "the process of creating solutions to human problems through creativity and the application of math and science knowledge" (10). They identify six elements in this process: defining a problem, researching possible solutions, choosing and planning the best solution, building and testing a prototype, improving a design, and communicating the solution. In simpler terms, the authors refer to "Think about it. Try it. Fix it. Share it" (6). In the playful STEM environment, open-ended, everyday materials can be picked up, examined, moved around, put together, taken apart, and put back together or transformed. Materials of different textures encourage children to learn about absorbency, color, flexibility, hardness, and other properties. Preschool teachers can even dedicate a makerspace in the classroom or shared space with other teachers where children creatively tinker, design, invent, and build, often in collaboration with others. Tinkering includes unstructured time to explore and invent, testing ideas and learning from mistakes. Time to "just" tinker reflects belief in the competency of children and trust that they can productively engage in risk-taking with these materials. These are some materials for preschoolers to tinker with in a makerspace:

- washers, nuts, bolts, screws, clamps

- cork, cardboard, toilet paper and paper towel tubes, egg cartons, packing materials

- small tiles

- magnets

- pipe cleaners, twist ties, bendable straws

- masking tape, duct tape, different-colored tapes, scissors, hole puncher, stapler, glue

- string, yarn, pom-poms, cotton balls, beads, buttons, fabric scraps, and developmentally appropriate sewing materials

- toothpicks, Popsicle sticks, craft sticks, wire

- paper clips, clothespins and clamps, string and yarn

- clay

- sketch pads for planning designs and redesigns

- wood scraps, old tires, and pieces of lumber for a supervised outdoor makerspace, as in the Anchorage Park Kindergarten

Math: Figure It Out!

As Betty Zan (Counsell et al. 2016) defines it, "Mathematics [is] equated with number and quantity, and special emphasis is placed on learning how to count" (4). For early childhood education, Zan focuses on the "study of number, quantity, and space" (5). Giving children everyday, playful items encourages them to identify numerals, count objects, estimate quantities, measure using their own devices (hands, feet, sticks, string, and so on), problem solve everyday situations (such as making sure everyone gets equal amounts), and make up their own counting games. Matching and sorting items according to size, color, shape, or texture helps children recognize and discover patterns. Patterns are the building blocks of science and math. Children learn to notice a pattern, recreate the pattern, look for missing parts to a pattern, extend a pattern, and create their own patterns. Mathematical skills support science, technology, and engineering. Here are some common materials to have on hand:

- dice

- playing cards

- bingo cards

- counting objects (buttons, toy figures, craft sticks, and so forth)

- coins

- calendar

- measuring tape, measuring cups, measuring spoons

- writing paper

- pencil, marker

- calculator

- charts and graphs for recording tallies and data

- materials for pattern investigations: acorns, shells, pebbles, leaves, buttons, beads, glass beads or gems, toy figures and cars, little colored or different-sized blocks and tiles

Early childhood teachers typically work with very limited budgets. However, we have found that stocking a STEM-centered environment does not have to be costly. Teachers can bring everyday items from home or find them in nature, families can donate or loan items, and yard sales and local businesses and organizations can yield recycled materials. On a study trip to Reggio Emilia, I visited REMIDA (the Creative Recycling Centre), where educators stroll with their shopping carts to pick and choose from discarded materials donated by local businesses. Several centers I have worked with stocked their paper supplies with leftovers or "ends" from the local newspaper office. Libraries and museums often loan early childhood programs kits to use for STEM investigations.

> **Self-Assessment Checklist**
>
> - What materials do you already have that support science learning? What else do you need to get started?
>
> - What materials do you already have that support technology learning? What else do you need to get started?
>
> - What materials do you already have that support engineering learning? What else do you need to get started?
>
> - What materials do you already have that support math learning? What else do you need to get started?
>
> - What materials can you and your colleagues share?
>
> - What can families donate? What can local businesses donate?
>
> - Is there a local recycling resource center?
>
> - Are there small grants available that you (perhaps with a colleague) can write proposals to secure funds for necessary materials?
>
> - Can you visit children's museums and libraries, or can you borrow materials from them?

One Thing to Try Tomorrow

Get paper and a pencil, sit down in your favorite chair, and relax with coffee or tea. Brainstorm a list of materials you'd love to have in your setting. Keep in mind your evolving philosophy to make sure you have your eye on the prize—STEM materials that include natural items and will support playful

inquiry and investigations. Don't reject any ideas yet—write down every-
thing you might desire. Then consider your target audience, people who
might actually read your list and consider a donation or some kind of sup-
port. Work your networks! Who might donate or spread the word? Families?
Friends? Professional organizations? Social media? Local businesses? The
library? A recycling center? Put together a quick, inviting request explaining
why you need these items. Proofread it, and then send out a quick email or
posting. Don't procrastinate—just do it!

Snapshot: Elisabeth Amen Nursery School

Family volunteers helped update the Amen outdoor environment.

For the past two years, the Amen School has focused on transforming its traditional playground into an invit-ing, inquiry-based outdoor classroom. Children, staff, and families now plant, tend, study, and document living things in their garden. Car-rying buckets of water from the water pump, they "cook and eat" in their mud kitchen. After their outdoor stage is refurbished, children will also share their poems, writings, songs, and music with peers and family members. Working at the outdoor easel, children enjoy an inspiring space to imagine and create. In this evolving STEM/STEAM environment, problem solving, inquiry-based learn-ing, the arts, and the 6Cs flourish. With help from families, community volunteers, and college students, this new environment is revitalized using materials that were donated, recycled, and repurposed, or sometimes bought through fundrais-ing (such as the outdoor easel). Favorite materials include muffin pans, strainers, metal spoons, bowls and pots in all sizes, wire whisks, measuring cups, turkey basters, shovels, garden spades, and buckets.

Snapshot: Local Head Start Program

Head Start teachers posted documentation from the class's study of clothing.

During a recent study of clothing, teachers and parents provided various materials, including corduroy, velour, cotton, rubber (found in raincoats), silk, wool, threads, yarn, and ribbons. Though the study was part of the required Head Start curriculum, the materials and clothing the families contributed broadened and deepened the scope of the investigations. Comparing and contrasting fabrics, children thought critically about properties of the materials. Children tinkered with buttons, snaps, zippers, hooks, Velcro, needles, and scissors to discover how they work. Parent volunteers modeled sewing and weaving and brought Saudi Arabian and Asian Indian dress from their home countries. Children also focused on the STEM skills of sorting and classifying items, discovering patterns in the fabrics, designing their own apparel, and learning to sew.

Snapshot: Anchorage Park Kindergarten

Believing that children are capable and competent, the Anchorage Park Kindergarten integrates their exploration of technology in a variety of thoughtful ways. The head teacher states that "sewing is technology that both the children and their families love!" Each week a parent volunteer assists children with both hand and machine sewing. The children and families love the idea that their grandparents (born in the 1950s and 1960s) relied on sewing their own clothing! Children use an older computer that is not internet connected but offers a photo booth, educational games, books, and movie clips. Practicing with the Kid Pix art program, using the mouse, sharing and taking turns, learning the basics of how a computer works, and showing respect for the opportunity to work at the computer, they can earn the Rainbow License for computer use. It's considered a high honor to earn the cherished Rainbow License, and children are recognized and celebrated during a presentation with their families. Once they have been awarded their license, they can use a computer with a printer or a tablet (with teacher support).

CHAPTER 7:
THE TEACHER'S ROLE IN THE STEM-CENTERED LEARNING ENVIRONMENT

The metaphor is that of a journey into unknown territory where a compass is the most useful instrument. The feelings belong to the children: curiosity, wonder, enthusiasm for the unknown. The courage necessary for this journey lies in the courage to choose, to make mistakes, and to be uncertain.

—Carlina Rinaldi, "Staff Development in Reggio Emilia," in *Reflections on the Reggio Emilia Approach*

In moving from a more traditional preschool setting to a Reggio-inspired STEM environment, the role of the teacher often shifts. Ask yourself whether your vision of your role reflects your evolving philosophy. Reimagining the environment cannot happen without affecting how the teacher views their role and the values and the messages they hope to convey to children and families. From my studies in Reggio Emilia and my work with preschool teachers, I have found that most often teachers' pedagogical emphases will shift in six particular areas, the focus of this chapter.

1. Pedagogy of Listening. Teachers committed to playful inquiry, the scientific processes, and STEM investigations allow for flexibility in their day and welcome children's questions as stepping-stones to possible STEM studies. This reflects what is known in Reggio Emilia as the pedagogy of listening, and it requires that teachers develop their skills in asking open-ended questions.

2. Documentation. Teachers committed to a Reggio-inspired STEM environment improve their documentation, which reveals children's learning while evoking further questions and reflection.

3. Background Knowledge. Understanding their role as co-researchers alongside the children, teachers build their own background knowledge on the question being studied as they allow STEM studies to evolve.

4. Early Literacy. During complex STEM investigations, the teacher embraces endless opportunities to support early literacy skills, particularly those associated with vocabulary.

5. Modeling Dispositions. Teachers in a playful, Reggio-inspired STEM environment understand the critical importance of modeling the dispositions they hope children will acquire: wonder, curiosity, critical thinking, and joyful learning with others.

6. Advocacy. Advocating for change typically requires administrative or outside support; thus, teachers need to be able to articulate their informed rationale for change, the value to their children, and what they require to make change happen.

The Pedagogy of Listening

The Reggio philosophy emphasizes the "pedagogy of listening," whereby teachers are attuned to children's questions, observations, misconceptions, and interests. Fighting the pressure to know the right answer, follow the scripted curriculum, and develop prescribed themes, Reggio educators take their cues from the children to plan investigations. Listening also requires careful observation, noticing what children are chatting about, pointing out, puzzled by, frustrated by, and so on.

As teachers, we are trained to ask endless questions, but most often our questions either elicit a yes or no response or seek the "right" answer. Of course there are times when this is important and necessary. However, sometimes this questioning technique backfires when it shuts down further discussion and elaboration instead of promoting or scaffolding discussion and critical thinking. Thus, in the inquiry-based STEM environment, teachers must develop their skills in opening up the discussion to solicit diverse perspectives, help children learn from one another, weigh next steps, and ultimately build a collective body of knowledge.

Increasing our skills in asking open-ended questions is challenging for many of us—so much so that one of the teachers in my class conducted her study for the course on assessing volunteer teachers' skills in asking open-ended questions. Using the data collected, she then worked with them to improve this skill. Effective teachers want to know *why* children make a particular comment (wrong or right), what they notice, how they might do something differently, and so on. Skillful teachers also respectfully challenge children's assumptions to prod their thinking. Which of these questions do you already ask or might you start asking? Some teachers post similar lists of question stems in their rooms to remind themselves (and the children) of productive questions to ask.

Self-Assessment Checklist

- What surprised you?

- What do you think would happen if _____?

- Why do you think that?

- How can you tell?

- What else do you need to know?

- Why are there _____?

- What happened when?

- How do we know?

- What did we do?

- What made us think?

- What could you do?

- Is there a way to _____?

- I wonder if I _____?

The attentive practice of listening, observing, and questioning helps teachers decide how to support the children's investigations. After carefully listening to children's comments, teachers prompt their thinking with cues and hints as well as with questions. Listening to children's responses helps teachers determine provocations that might further their interests, puzzle them, or deepen their thinking. For example, children amazed by a rainbow after a rainstorm might ask how rainbows are made. Noticing the children's wonder and listening to their comments, the teacher might ask, "How would you describe the rainbow? How do you think rainbows are made? How could we try to make a rainbow? What would we need to do? What materials might we use to make a rainbow? Why would we use those materials?" The next day, the teacher might bring to class crystal prisms or a flashlight and a glass of water as provocations, initiating a deeper study.

Documentation

Integral to the Reggio philosophy is the practice of documentation, capturing aha moments through children's drawings, children's language, photos, videos, creations, and so on. Teachers who are new to documentation are encouraged to view themselves as archaeologists mining pivotal moments in children's developing understanding: their questions, confusions, stumbling blocks, explanations, drawings, constructions, discoveries. Documentation preserves the story of the project, which can then be shared and celebrated with the children, families, and the community. Contemplating *why* certain determinations or decisions were made encourages critical thinking in children. With teacher scaffolding, they can begin to look for patterns, misunderstandings, comparisons, and contrasts as to why one thing happened rather than another. Documentation is also a powerful tool for representing the developing 6Cs as children collaborate, communicate, create, think critically about rich content, and grow in confidence during their STEM investigations.

As I point out to teachers, starting small is important to developing any new practice or habit. Learning to document takes time and greatly benefits from collegial support, as is regularly practiced by Reggio educators. The Amen School teachers often chat over lunch, sharing their ongoing documentation efforts, soliciting feedback and suggestions, and bouncing around ideas for possible next steps. A good starting point in trying more robust documentation is to use children's drawings. Adding quotes from the children captures their questions, surprises, and new learning. Including teacher notes conveys bumps along the way and discusses next steps. Photo panels likewise make learning visible. As Carla Neumann-Hinds notes in *Picture Science*, "[Photos] are very helpful in reminding children *what* they did and in prompting them to think about *why* they did it" (2007, 64–65). I find video documentation the most useful, and when coupled with the other artifacts of learning, it allows everyone to revisit events and pause or rewind for further reflection.

Background Knowledge

Nearly all teachers ask how important it is for the teacher to have background knowledge in topics of interest to the children. The teachers at the Elisabeth Amen School, my local Head Start, and Anchorage Park Kindergarten agree that teachers, as researchers themselves alongside the children, need to expand their STEM background knowledge: rainbows, shadows, tadpoles, reflections, speed, construction, and so on. Although "the quality of science learning experiences provided to young children directly corresponds to teachers' science content knowledge" (Marx and Harris 2006, as cited by Counsell et al. 2016, 159), most preschool teachers have limited coursework or preparation in the STEM areas. To gain this knowledge requires time—time that is precious to already overloaded preschool teachers. Happily, there are many informal ways to increase STEM knowledge without taking additional courses or training:

- collaborating with colleagues (virtually or in person) through a community of practice or professional learning group

- starting or joining a book club with other preschool teachers

- accessing online sites and networks of like-minded colleagues

- messing about with materials or loose parts with colleagues

- observing an admired colleague or viewing photos or videos together, then asking questions

- planning "one step for tomorrow" with a colleague

Starting with an area in which you already have background knowledge provides a confident springboard into a STEM investigation. Perhaps you play a musical instrument, collect shells, or spend time on DIY projects, cooking, or gardening—all STEM-related hobbies that you can bring to your setting. As you work alongside the children, responding to their questions, you will also expand your background knowledge. We won't always know the answers or have adequate background knowledge, but modeling the authentic dispositions of curiosity and willingness to learn alongside the children reinforces the value we place in the inquiry model.

Early Literacy

Teachers and I discuss the importance of modeling and extending children's vocabulary authentically, in context. Building children's vocabulary in a meaningful and appropriate way contributes to their developing background knowledge and future academic success. Building vocabulary in context, rather than in isolation, is particularly important for English learners. During playful investigations, children begin to build schemas or organized relationships between connected vocabulary terms that will serve them well in their later schooling.

Opportunities to enhance children's vocabulary abound throughout the STEM environment. In addition to the enriching vocabulary in STEM-related books, consider all the terminology used just in investigations about balls and ramps: speed, size, incline, friction, motion, momentum, distance. Or consider investigations about plants: seeds, growth, change, seed-lings, roots, stem, leaves, buds, petals, blossoms, and decay. The possibilities are endless!

Modeling Dispositions

Modeling dispositions is probably the teacher's most important role in the playful, inquiry-based STEM environment. Imagine children's excitement when they see their teacher enthusiastic, surprised, confused, stumped, curious, or wondrous! Your attitude is contagious, as young children are easily influenced by their teachers and often want to be like them. If you are curious about what lives in the water at the nearby pond, they will share your excitement. If you are amazed at the tall trees in the woods on your nature walk, they will share your wonder, asking how the trees got so big, how old the trees are, why there are pine needles on the ground, where the pine cones come from, and why the tree fell down.

Advocacy

Finally, Reggio teachers view their role not only as educators but also as advocates, advocating for the rights of children, including the right to learn together in an environment that serves as the third teacher. When visiting Reggio Emilia, Italy, I was in awe of their relentless commitment to their philosophy and the leadership they showed in transforming their programs to convey their messages and values. To accomplish change requires a keen understanding of the decision-making culture and politics of your particular program to find support for your evolving philosophy (particularly if you work in a program with multiple classrooms and teachers). If the advocacy role is new or intimidating for you, start by taking one baby step and, when possible, do so in collaboration with like-minded and supportive colleagues.

Self-Assessment Checklist

- What is the decision-making culture of your school? How and where can you find support?

- What kind of professional learning works best for you (working together with colleagues, online networks, book clubs, taking courses)?

- Where would you like to start? What interests you at this time? What small step can you take first?

- Would it be helpful to attend a workshop or a conference, or to invite someone in with helpful expertise?

- Do you have a hobby or skill that you can use as a springboard for STEM learning and risk-taking in your classroom (photography, cooking, sewing, crafting, gardening, bird-watching, playing a musical instrument, repairing things)?

One Thing to Try Tomorrow

A quick strategy I have found to be extremely effective in improving teaching skills is scripting. Scripting provides a quick snapshot and informal assessment to help determine goals for improving your practice. Choose a question of interest regarding your teaching. Perhaps you want to collect data about the kinds of questions you most often ask or your use of rich STEM vocabulary with the children. Use your phone to self-record for a few minutes or ask a nonjudgmental colleague, intern, or classroom volunteer to jot down (or record on their phone or tablet) a list of questions that you ask (or STEM vocabulary you use) during a five- or ten-minute time frame (or whatever time frame works best for you). Then analyze your data. Categorize your questions: for example, were they most often soliciting right or wrong answers, or was there a mix of open-ended questions promoting critical thinking? This will give you a baseline for considering next steps, such as posting question stems on the wall or door. Perhaps your colleague will do the same, and you can compare notes, set goals, monitor your progress, and support one another.

Snapshot: Elisabeth Amen Nursery School

Amen teachers have found that focusing on creating documentation of children's investigations has spurred their own critical thinking. Additionally, they agree that documentation preserves the story of the project, which can then be shared and celebrated with the children, families, and the community.

The new director at the Amen School describes their ongoing process of change, including the positive impact on their professional development and teaching roles. She notes that the team of teachers "figures out together" how they will try out something new and challenging: "Being afraid doesn't stop us— we still take many risks." To determine their goals, they examine what research says about outdoor learning environments and consider what would be sustainable and available within their limited budget. Once a change is underway, they evaluate what is working and what is not.

The outdoor learning environment provides for more intentional observations of children. As the director explains, "We set aside time for observation. I like to take little notes on index cards. The other teacher has a notebook for each child. A third teacher has portfolios and index cards. We even decided to take an observation course together." Documentation gathered during brief teacher observations revealed teachers' growing insights into their pedagogy of listening and questioning skills. In collaboration with the director, teachers analyzed the scripts of their interactions with children and teased out the questions and vocabulary they were using. In Reggio style, thinking about questioning has now become a topic of their weekly professional development meetings. As the director notes, "We have discovered that, for us, learning to document is a challenging process. As we struggle to provoke, reframe, and revisit, we ask ourselves what we are looking for. We were surprised and didn't expect that learning to document would provoke such critical thinking on our part."

Snapshot: Local Head Start Program

Since their STEM study began, the director describes the teachers as "more intentional" in their questioning skills and documentation efforts. She notes that in her observations, the teachers are more self-aware of the level of their questioning and using more open-ended questions. Walking through their hallways, one is struck by their photos telling the stories of a recent study. Families are invited in to celebrate and share their children's learning through the documentation. The director describes some teachers as finding that the "light bulb went on" for them in sparking playful STEM investigations. Of particular value to the teachers in refining their professional roles has been using the GOLD Documentation app on their tablets. They have found this much more user friendly for observing, planning, assessing, and documenting than having sticky notes or binders for each child. For example, when children see an insect and start to ask questions, the teachers can immediately use the tablet to look up the insect, find information, and take photos. At the same time, the app allows them to note which children showed interest, as well as their observations and the vocabulary they used, and assess their current level of performance to share with families.

Snapshot: Anchorage Park Kindergarten

Paper portfolios from Anchorage Park Kindergarten

The head teacher suggested that this chapter, focusing on the role of the teacher, is the most important chapter and should be first in the book because, as she states, "None of what we have discussed will happen without the teacher!" This recommendation reflects her respect for the expertise, perspectives, and contributions of her staff, while together, in Reggio fashion, they worked toward implementing their philosophy.

Her teachers have become more intentional in their decision-making and have spent time considering the value of digital and paper portfolios. Although her staff finds value in digital portfolios, they find more benefits in creating hands-on, paper portfolios with the children. With digital portfolios, children may have hundreds of photos to sort through. But when children can hold their very own portfolio or book of memories, the head teacher states that they "revisit their own journeys and their memories of childhood" with friends and families. Sitting on their family member's lap, they can together remember important events in their lives from the year. This documentation supports revisiting and reflection and creates moments of celebration and connectedness. Creating meaningful documentation requires the teachers to become keen listeners and astute observers to capture the wondrous, magical moments of the children's days.

The Anchorage Park Kindergarten develops an annual plan that sets goals for the upcoming year. After all the assessments have been completed, including surveys from families, the team determines their plan for the upcoming year. During the year, the team meets weekly. Recently, their focus has been on the role of the teacher and how to strengthen "intentional" teaching. Commenting on these planning meetings, the head teacher notes that their purpose is "to be reflective, to challenge ourselves, to consider teaching strategies and learning outcomes— an ongoing self-assessment moving us forward as to what needs to change."

CHAPTER 8:
RESOURCES FOR SETTING UP A REGGIO-INSPIRED STEM ENVIRONMENT

Getting started setting up a Reggio-inspired STEM environment is easier than you might think. There are endless resources for teachers who are interested in finding one thing to try tomorrow. In this chapter, I have included a sampling of useful websites, helpful professional development books, some high-quality children's STEM books, and a listing of STEM standards and position papers. Most of these resources are free to access; however, some do involve purchases or subscriptions. (Please note that I have no financial affiliation with these resources, which come highly recommended by other educators.) They are user friendly, designed for busy teachers who have limited time for their own professional development. Checking out just one of these will get you started with enthusiasm.

Websites and Apps

Alliance for Childhood: https://allianceforchildhood.org
This website promotes child-initiated, open-ended play opportunities and play networks to improve the lives of children. Inspiring photos and videos of children are showcased along with tools for advocating for the benefits of children's play.

Education Development Center (EDC): www.edc.org
The EDC is a global nonprofit and a leader in developing innovative programs around the world. Their resources include tool kits, apps, books, and curricula.

EiE (Engineering Is Elementary): www.eie.org/stem-curricula/engineering-grades-prek-8 /wee-engineer
This Wee Engineer section of the EiE website introduces teachers to hands-on engineering challenges for young children. Through project-based learning, preschoolers (like adult engineers) attempt to solve problems. This site is also loaded with digital resources for preschool teachers and families.

Engaging Children in STEM: http://resourcesforearlylearning.org/educators/module/20/16
This website module provides three videos for early childhood educators to explore best
    practices for teaching STEM. Participants observe and reflect on strategies to scaffold
    children's new learning.

GOLD Documentation by Teaching Strategies: https://teachingstrategies.com/solutions
/assess/gold
This app, used by the Head Start program featured in this book, provides tools for teachers to
    collect and organize data quickly, including online portfolios. Reports can be shared with
    families. In particular, this program addresses the learning needs of children with special
    needs and those whose first language is not English. (A subscription is needed.)

Growing Book by Book: https://growingbookbybook.com
This website dedicates sections to young children's math and science books.

KinderLab Robotics: https://kinderlabrobotics.com
This website focuses on "Build. Art. Code. Play." Teacher resources include newsletters,
    blogs, videos, activities, and trainings.

North American Reggio Emilia Alliance: www.reggioalliance.org/narea
As a member of the Reggio Children International Network, the North American Reggio
    Emilia Alliance connects early childhood educators and advocates through conferences,
    networking, and resource sharing.

Preschool STEAM: https://preschoolsteam.com/science-activities-preschoolers
This user-friendly website provides preschool teachers with STEAM (science, technology,
    engineering, arts, and mathematics) experiences that spur curiosity, with steps for
    creating and integrating STEAM opportunities into any setting.

Reggio Children: www.reggiochildren.it/en
On this website, the Reggio Emilia approach is described as an "ecosystem of content and
    strategies" provided by live webinars, courses, videos, and online publishing. Here you can
    view photos and videos from Reggio centers. It also provides information about partici-
    pating in study groups related to Reggio Emilia.

TRUCE (Teachers Resisting Unhealthy Children's Development): www.truceteachers.org
Developed by early childhood educators, this website promotes the importance of children's
    play. It offers free and downloadable resources, including family play plans, STEM play
    guides, toy selection guides, and other resources for those interested in less technology
    and more high-quality play. (I am a steering committee member.)

Videative Series: https://videatives.com/company
In Reggio fashion, Videative's mission is to make children's thinking visible. They do this
    through short video clips with supporting text, many of which focus on playful, inquiry-
    based STEM experiences. The videos support teachers in understanding what children
    know and scaffolding new learning.

Children's Books

- *Bright Beetle* by Rick Chrustowski

- *Butterflies* by Seymour Simon

- *Charlotte the Scientist Is Squished* by Camille Andros

- *A House Is a House for Me* by Mary Ann Hoberman

- *Jump, Frog, Jump!* by Robert Kalan

- *Keepers of Life: Discovering Plants through Native American Stories and Earth Activities for Children* by Michael J. Caduto and Joseph Bruchac

- *Mama Robot* by Davide Cali

- *The Most Magnificent Thing* by Ashley Spires

- *Mrs. Spitzer's Garden* by Edith Pattou

- *Newton and Me* by Lynne Mayer

- *A Perfect Day for Digging* by Cari Best

- *Stems* by Melanie Mitchell

- *A Stick Is an Excellent Thing: Poems Celebrating Outdoor Play* by Marilyn Singer

- *Violet the Pilot* by Steve Breen

- *What Do You Do with an Idea?* by Kobi Yamada

- *What to Do with a Box* by Jane Yolen

- *Yucky Worms* by Vivian French

Professional Books

- *Blocks and Beyond: Strengthening Early Math and Science Skills through Spatial Learning* by Mary Jo Pollman

- *Experiencing Nature with Young Children: Awakening Delight, Curiosity, and a Sense of Stewardship* by Alice Sterling Honig

- *Loose Parts: Inspiring Play in Young Children* by Lisa Daly and Miriam Beloglovsky

- *Making and Tinkering with STEM: Solving Design Challenges with Young Children* by Cate Heroman

- *Nature-Based Learning for Young Children: Anytime, Anywhere, on Any Budget* by Julie Powers and Sheila Williams Ridge (See appendix 2 for children's STEM books, appendix 3 for resources for adults, and appendix 5 for materials, supplies, and equipment.)

- *Serious Fun: How Guided Play Extends Children's Learning*, edited by Marie L. Masterson and Holly Bohart

- *Starting with Science: Strategies for Introducing Young Children to Inquiry* by Marcia Talhelm Edson

- *Worms, Shadows, and Whirlpools: Science in the Early Childhood Classroom* by Karen Worth and Sharon Grollman

Position Papers and Standards

Position statements are an important tool that the National Association for the Education of Young Children (NAEYC) uses to build understanding and support for significant issues related to early childhood education. They are written by consensus and revised as needed. The first link below will take you to the main page for position papers, followed by specific links to position statements related to science, math, and technology.

NAEYC Position Statements: www.naeyc.org/resources/position-statements

Math: "Executive Summary: Early Childhood Mathematics: Promoting Good Beginnings"
www.naeyc.org/sites/default/files/globally-shared/downloads/PDFs/resources/position
-statements/Mathematics_Exec.pdf

Science: "Early Childhood Science Education"
www.naeyc.org/sites/default/files/globally-shared/downloads/PDFs/resources/position
-statements/Early%20Childhood%20FINAL%20FINAL%201-30-14%20%281%29%20
%281%29.pdf

Technology: "Technology and Interactive Media as Tools in Early Childhood Programs Serving Children from Birth through Age 8"
www.naeyc.org/resources/topics/technology-and-media/resources

REFERENCES

Bartolini, Vicki, and E. Patrick Rashleigh. 2017. "Transforming a Reggio-Inspired Documentation Assignment Using VoiceThread, an Online Collaborative Tool." *Innovations in Early Education: The International Reggio Emilia Exchange* 24 (1): 14–23. www.reggioalliance.org/wp-content/uploads/2017/03/Innov.24.1web.pdf.

Counsell, Shelly, Lawrence Escalada, Rosemary Geiken, Melissa Sander, Jill Uhlenberg, Beth Van Meeteren, Sonia Yoshizawa, and Betty Zan. 2016. *STEM Learning with Young Children: Inquiry Teaching with Ramps and Pathways*. New York: Teachers College Press.

De Arment, Sara, Yaoying Xu, and Heather Coleman. 2016. "Optimizing Accessibility through Universal Design for Learning." In *Environment: Promoting Meaningful Access, Participation, and Inclusion*, edited by Tricia Catalino and Lori E. Meyer, 33–50. Washington, DC: Division for Early Childhood.

Donohue, Chip, and Roberta Schomberg. 2017. "Technology and Interactive Media in Early Childhood Programs: What We've Learned from Five Years of Research, Policy, and Practice." *Young Children* 72 (4). www.naeyc.org/resources/pubs/yc/sep2017/technology-and-interactive-media.

Edwards, Carolyn, Lella Gandini, and George Forman, eds. 2012. *The Hundred Languages of Children: The Reggio Emilia Experience in Transformation*. 3rd ed. Santa Barbara, CA: Praeger.

Fyfe, Brenda. 1994. "Images from the United States: Using Ideas from the Reggio Emilia Experience with American Educators." In *Reflections on the Reggio Emilia Approach*, edited by Lilian G. Katz and Bernard Cesarone, 19–32. Urbana, IL: ERIC Clearinghouse on Elementary and Early Childhood Education. https://files.eric.ed.gov/fulltext/ED375986.pdf.

———. 2019. "Review of *Border Crossings: Encounters with Living Things/Digital Landscapes*." *Innovations in Early Education: The International Reggio Emilia Exchange* 26 (4): 38–39. www.reggioalliance.org/wp-content/uploads/2020/01/NAR19_Innovations_264_Web_low.pdf.

Gandini, Lella. 2012. "Connecting through Caring and Learning Spaces." In *The Hundred Languages of Children: The Reggio Emilia Experience in Transformation*, 3rd ed. edited by Carolyn Edwards, Lella Gandini, and George Forman, 317–42. Santa Barbara, CA: Praeger.

Golinkoff, Roberta Michnick, and Kathy Hirsh-Pasek. 2016. *Becoming Brilliant: What Science Tells Us about Raising Successful Children*. Washington, DC: American Psychological Association.

Hirsh-Pasek, Kathy, Roberta Michnick Golinkoff, Laura E. Berk, and Dorothy G. Singer. 2009. *A Mandate for Playful Learning in Preschool: Presenting the Evidence*. New York: Oxford University Press.

Leonni, Leo. 2017. *Little Blue and Little Yellow*. Reprint ed. New York: Dragonfly Books.

Malaguzzi, Loris. (1987) 2015. *To Make a Portrait of a Lion*. DVD. Reggio Children USA.

Marshall, Nancy L., Julie Dennehy, Christine Johnson-Staub, and Wendy Wagner Robeson. 2005. *Massachusetts Capacity Study Research Brief: Characteristics of the Current Early Education and Care Workforce Serving 3–5 Year-Olds*. Wellesley, MA: Center for Research on Women, Wellesley College. https://files.eric.ed.gov/fulltext/ED495144.pdf.

Neumann-Hinds, Carla. 2007. *Picture Science: Using Digital Photography to Teach Young Children*. St. Paul, MN: Redleaf Press.

Rinaldi, Carlina. 1994. "Staff Development in Reggio Emilia." In *Reflections on the Reggio Emilia Approach*, edited by Lilian G. Katz and Bernard Cesarone, 55–60. Urbana, IL: ERIC Clearinghouse on Elementary and Early Childhood Education. https://files.eric.ed.gov/fulltext/ED375986.pdf.

Shaw, Charles G. 2014. *It Looked Like Spilt Milk*. New York: HarperFestival.

Stacey, Susan. 2019. *Inquiry-Based Early Learning Environments: Creating, Supporting, and Collaborating*. St. Paul, MN: Redleaf Press.

Stone-MacDonald, Angi, Kristen Wendell, Anne Douglass, and Mary Lu Love. 2015. *Engaging Young Engineers: Teaching Problem-Solving Skills through STEM*. Baltimore, MD: Paul H. Brookes.